Children Speak

Children, Trauma and Social Work

'01

Other titles from Longman include:

NSPCC: *Child Sexual Abuse: Listening, Hearing and Validating the Experiences of Children* by Corinne Wattam, John Hughes and Harry Blagg

NSPCC: *Listening to Children: The Professional Response to Hearing the Abused Child* edited by Anne Bannister, Kevin Barrett and Eileen Shearer

NSPCC: *From Hearing to Healing: Working with the Aftermath of Child Sexual Abuse* edited by Anne Bannister

NSPCC: *Making a Case in Child Protection* by Corinne Wattam

NSPCC: *Key Issues in Child Protection for Health Visitors and Nurses* edited by Jane Naish and Christopher Cloke

Female Sexual Abuse of Children: the Ultimate Taboo edited by Michele Elliott

Making Sense of the Children Act (2nd edition) by Nick Allen

Social Services Training Manuals

First Line Management: Staff by Kevin Ford and Sarah Hargreaves

Effective Use of Teambuilding by Alan Dearling

Manual on Elder Abuse by Chris Phillipson and Simon Biggs

Developing Training Skills by Tim Pickles, Howie Armstrong and Bruce Britton

Training for Mental Health by Thurstine Basset and Elaine Burrel

Monitoring and Evaluation in the Social Services by David and Suzanne Thorpe

Child Protection Training Manual by Brenda Green, Sissi Loftin and Paul Saunders

Quest for Equality by Errol John and Barbara Deering

Care Sector Quality: a training manual incorporating BS5750 by Steve Casson and Clive George

Children Speak
Children, Trauma and Social Work

by

Ian Butler and Howard Williamson

LONGMAN

Published by Longman Information and Reference,
Longman Group Limited, 6th Floor, Westgate House, The High,
Harlow, Essex CM20 1YR, England and Associated Companies
throughout the world.

© Longman Group Limited 1994

A catalogue record for this book is available from The British
Library

ISBN 0–582–25330–6

Typeset by Fakenham Photosetting Ltd,
Fakenham, Norfolk

Printed in Great Britain by BPC Wheatons Ltd, Exeter

For
Mark, Daniel,
Matthew, Rebecca, Thomas,
Daniel, Martyn and Morgan

Acknowledgements

We have kept much of the pleasure of writing this book to ourselves but we have been liberal with our miseries and problems. By way of recompense, albeit inadequate, to all of those whose ideas we have used and on whom we have imposed, we would like to record particular thanks to Murray Davies of the NSPCC, a man who really knows and cares about children; to Neil Hopkins, also of the NSPCC, particularly for the last chapter and for encouraging our belief that what we had to say did have a practical application; to our colleagues within the School of Social and Administrative Studies in Cardiff, to Paul Atkinson and Sara Delamont for their genuine interest, unfailing enthusiasm and active engagement; particularly Ian Shaw for his personal and professional support; to all of those who facilitated access to the young people with whom we spoke, to Alan Dearling, our publisher; to our own partners and children (this is what we were doing when we were too busy to pay you much attention) and most of all to the young people who, after all, are the real authors here.

Ian Butler
Howard Williamson
Cardiff

Contents

Foreword

Over 200 years ago the Government of the United States adopted the Declaration of the Rights of Man, leading to fears in England at the time that next would come thoughts about *the rights of youngsters, children and babies*. It has taken a long time to introduce into an international treaty the principle that children have civil rights, which is enshrined in the UN Convention on the Rights of the Child, adopted by the UN General Assembly in 1989. Even now the case of children's rights is not without controversy, and following the Convention, and the Children Act 1989 in England and Wales, the debate about the balance between parents and children's rights continues. Some people argue that the balance has already swung too far in favour of children's rights, but the changes that have taken place have had little impact on children's status in society, and restrictions to effective participation, and self-determination remain.

Within this debate the NSPCC remains a *strong, national, independent and challenging voice for children*, a position restated by the Society's Council in adopting a radical new strategy for the 1990s which confirms the Society's commitment to use its experience and expertise to focus on the needs of children. Such a focus requires new partnerships with children, in which their views are expressed and listened to, so that they can influence service development and provision. The right to participate in decisions which affect them is one of the fundamental rights enshrined in the Convention. Listening to children, and developing partnerships is important, and can be difficult to achieve, but the process is important if children are to be accepted as people in their own right.

The importance of listening to children has been highlighted in recent NSPCC national campaigns and publications, directed to adults as parents, and as providers of services to children. The importance of being informed by children is confirmed by other research which demonstrates that children's perceptions as users and recipients of services are influenced by different considerations to the professionals who provide them, resulting in different conclusions. If we are to serve children effectively, we must be prepared to listen and learn from what children have to say to us.

In the field of child protection, the child's view has been significantly absent. Indeed, policy, law, and practice have been developed from adult's views of the needs of vulnerable children. Major inquiries have, for decades, acted as catalysts for new policies or procedures following tragic occurrences, but consultation with children about their views of their needs has not received the same investment of time and resources. In all of this there is the danger of adults perpetuating a protective model in relation to children which inhibits the recognition of children's real capacity to participate.

This book marks a very significant shift in approach, made possible by changes within the NSPCC, which quite simply put children at the centre of the Society's work. We wish to understand need from a child's perspective, and as this book demonstrates there are some very important lessons for all adults.

The research commissioned by the NSPCC from the University of Wales in Cardiff was to secure children's views of *harm, risk, and their anxieties*, and the sort of support, advice or assistance they desired. This, it was intended, would provide a child-centred perspective on 'significant harm' as defined in the Children Act, and also inform the NSPCC about the real concerns and worries of children in the 1990s.

The results reported in this book challenge current professional understanding and practice, and suggests radical new child centred responses to helping children who are worried, and suffering harm. The children concerned are fairly critical of current practice, but can adults listen and learn from what is being said? This work demonstrates that children can clearly articulate their concerns, and evaluate levels of risk. Because these differ from adult perceptions, does this invalidate them, or does it confirm a need to *listen, respect, learn and take action?*

This work has already had an impact on NSPCC services, and this publication should cause all those working with children to review their practice. It also demonstrates a need for much more consultation with children.

Christopher Brown   Murray Davies
Director and Chief Executive   Regional Director
NSPCC   NSPCC Cymru/Wales and Midlands

1 Centuries of adulthood

The child thinks of growing old as an almost obscene calamity, which for some mysterious reason will never happen to itself. All who have passed the age of thirty are joyless grotesques, endlessly fussing about things of no importance and staying alive without, so far as the child can see, having anything to live for. Only child life is real life. (George Orwell, *A Collection of Essays*)

Childhood is only the beautiful and happy time in contemplation and retrospect: to the child it is full of deep sorrows, the meaning of which is unknown. (George Eliot, *George Eliot's Family Life and Letters*, Volume One, Arthur Paterson)

Introduction

These lines from Orwell and Eliot suggest a number of the themes that run through this book. First, both recognise that childhood is more than just quantitatively separated from adulthood by the passage of years. Childhood is also *qualitatively* different from adulthood. They reveal, moreover, that any conception of childhood, especially one's own, is constructed, in adulthood, quite differently to how it was experienced at the time. They remind us also that childhood is a serious business (Medrich *et al.* 1982).

This book is about children talking about aspects of their childhood. For much of the book, children speak directly about their lives, their 'worst experiences' and their dealings with adults. It is not enough, however, that children should speak; it is important that adults should listen too. For how adults understand childhood is a further important theme of this book. Indeed, the motivating force behind it was the desire to provide an opportunity for young people to speak, in their own words, directly to adults. Such opportunities have, historically, been few and far between. Children's accounts form only a minor part of the record of succeeding generations of children and childhood. The *heart* of *this* book is children's own accounts. Before moving on to hear what they have to say, however, this chapter explores some of the reasons why adults seldom listen or hear.

The social construction of childhood

Childhood is not a fixed and certain entity. After Aries' *Centuries of Childhood* (1960), few find the concept of the social construction of childhood controversial. The idea that childhood is culturally and generationally defined and re-defined is borne out by the experience of anyone with even the slightest awareness of social history. The life and times of those children who went off in the early part of the thirteenth century to fight in the Children's Crusade and who, in the main, were sold into slavery or who were press-ganged into the navy in the eighteenth century; or those children who were hanged at Tyburn following the Gordon riots or who pulled the wagons of coal to the surface only a matter of miles from where we write, in a time that our grandparents remember are fundamentally different to each other and fundamentally different to the life and times of children working today in Bangkok's brothels or the rag trade in South East London (see Pinchbeck and Hewitt 1973, Heywood 1969). That much is self-evident. What remains controversial is the particular construction of childhood that is regarded as ideal and the demography and aetiology of contemporary forms and experiences of childhood.

Throughout this book, we use the term 'childhood' to encompass all of that period which adults define as preceding the age of majority. Where we wish to distinguish between pre-teens and teenagers, we shall refer to 'children' and 'young people' respectively.

In relation to social work, the historical mutability of childhood is well attested to in the literature on juvenile delinquency, particularly in Pearson's seminal *Hooligan: A History of Respectable Fears* (Pearson 1983, see also Muncie 1984). In this, Pearson describes not only the history of youthful deviance but also describes the 'timeless phenomenon' of 'the grumbling of older generations against the folly of youth' (Pearson 1983, p.220).

Pearson's larger point is that the history of childhood is also very much the history of adults' myth-making around childhood, the point that George Eliot makes too. Childhood is often no more than what adults say it is. In this sense, all we have ever had is centuries of adulthood.

Despite significant criticisms of Aries (see Archard 1993), one important legacy of his work has been the recognition that the dominant contemporary construction of childhood in northern Europe implies a physical separation of children and adults at work and at play and a separation between adulthood and childhood as measured in psychological and emotional, as well as economic and cultural, terms.

The 'otherness' of children and childhood is reinforced culturally by a particular literature for and about childhood and by a considerable commercial investment aimed specifically at separating children from their pocket money.

We can associate this with a confident Western tradition of developmental psychology that describes the achievement of adulthood as the consummation of a sequential process of mastery (*sic*) and control and we have the foundations of a deficit model of childhood. Such a model of childhood has direct consequences for our understanding of children and the social world that they inhabit. For the separation of children and adults and of childhood and adulthood carries with it not only an assumption about the relative competence of children but also an assumption about their inferior status.

Child liberation

One particular account of and challenge to this separateness and implied subordination gained considerable currency in the writings of the 'child liberationists' of the 1970s.

Holt's 1975 child liberationist 'manifesto' *Escape from Childhood — The Needs and Rights of Children* describes the state of childhood as,

> being wholly subservient and dependent . . . being seen by others as a mixture of expensive nuisance, slave and super-pet (Holt 1975, p.15).

Holt goes on to describe family life as a 'training for slavery'. Even parental love is fuelled by less than disinterested motives. Children are, to their parents, no more than 'love objects' in the same way that women have been treated as sex objects. Adults, parents in particular, exploit children in that, in order to meet our own needs, we, think we have a right, or even a duty to bestow on [children] 'love' . . . whenever we want, however we want and whether they like it or not (*ibid*, p.80).

More recently Franklin's *The Rights of Children* (Franklin 1986) has given expression to the liberationist perspective in much more contemporary terms. He claims that,

the irrationality and immorality of systematic and institutionalised discrimination against individuals on the basis of their gender or race has, to degree, been established . . . equivalent discrimination against people on the basis of their age has proven more resilient to change (Franklin 1986, p.1).

This association of the emancipatory progress of women, ethnic minorities and other subordinated groups with the experience of childhood has produced some striking rhetoric around the contemporary lot of children in Western society. The American feminist Shulamith Firestone saw in the 'myth of childhood' a way for adults to compensate for all the things that either were or are missing in their lives:

. . . it is every parent's duty to give his child a childhood to remember (swing sets, inflated swimming pools, toys and games, camping trips, birthday parties, etc.). This is the Golden Age that the child will remember when he grows up to become a robot like his father . . . Young adults dream of having their own children in a desperate attempt to fill up the void produced by the artificial cutoff from the young . . . (Firestone 1979, p.40).

And she enjoins us to:

. . . talk about what childhood is really like and not of what it is like in adult heads . . . In a culture of alienated people, the belief that everyone has at least one good period in life free of care and drudgery dies hard. And obviously you can't expect it in old age. So it must be you've already had it. This accounts for the fog of sentimentality surrounding any discussion of childhood or children. Everyone is living out some private dream on their behalf . . . (*ibid*, p.42).

Consequently children are, according to Firestone:

. . . burdened with a wish fantasy in direct proportion to the restraints of their narrow lives; with an unpleasant sense of their own physical inadequacy and ridiculousness; with constant shame about their dependence, economic and otherwise ('Mother, may I?'); and humiliation concerning their natural ignorance of practical affairs. Children are repressed at every waking minute. Childhood is hell (*ibid*, p.50).

The limitations of the child liberationist perspective are well documented (Pollock 1983, Fox Harding 1991, Archard 1993). In our view, its proponents never fully resolve the central dilemma of arguing for continuity between childhood and adulthood and their essential similarities but all the time describing discontinuities and predicating difference. Similarly, the continuation of parental duties in the context of children's rights, which is universally implied, is contradictory. Moreover, taking this perspective to its logical conclusion, it re-presents the prospect and possibility of young children at work and at war. Such a prospect is repugnant to us.

Even so, while the criticisms of the child liberationists are sufficiently powerful for Fox Harding (1991) to describe the influence of liberationist thinking on public policy as 'marginal', there are elements of the liberationists' arguments that we feel are relevant to the central themes of this book.

We would agree that the cultural or ideological assumption of the 'otherness' of children may well owe more to the needs and wishes of adults than it does to the subjective experience of children or any objective assessment of their intellectual, emotional and social competence. As Archard (1993) argues:

We think of children as incapable by their very nature, and are disinclined to countenance the idea that they might be more competent than we presume. Moreover, the presumption retains its plausibility only by generalising across all childhood and ignoring the real differences between children of differing ages. Thinking of all children as incapable is credible when the contrast is between a helpless infant and an able-bodied adult. It is less so when it is a teenager who stands next to an adult (Archard 1993, p.68).

Similarly, we would agree that the assumption of relative competence is self-confirming. Without the opportunity and the space to practice the social, emotional and intellectual skills of decision-making, for example, children and young people will remain unskilled.

The precise point at which competences develop is too large a subject for these pages but our point in raising the issue is to forewarn against the cultural presumption that children and young people can have little or nothing to tell us either because they know little or nothing or because they do not understand.

We would suggest also that the rhetoric of 'rights-speak', which owes something of its origins to the liberationists, is a useful correc-

tive to any over reliance on 'needs-speak'. In describing the tension
that exists between self-determination and protection, Freeman
(1983) has noted, with perhaps unintentional irony, that:

> enhancing children's rights to protection from abuse, at least in
> the British context, has tended to diminish their autonomy
> (Freeman 1983, p.89).

Similarly we wish to warn against the presumption that we know
already what little it is that children may have to tell us. Your
childhood is not their childhood and your views on their childhood
may not correspond with their experience of it. In the pages that
follow, we present an image of childhood that may not correspond
either to your experience or your expectations but that, in itself, does
not provide grounds for discounting what the young people have to
say.

Children and the legacy of social work practice

> Tony Latham's intention in operation of Pin Down was to help
> the young people concerned . . . it was to provide intensive
> individualised programmes with the aim of dealing . . . with the
> child's problems.

As this statement, made in May 1991, by Tony Latham's solici-
tor (and quoted in Stone 1993), suggests few adult professionals
working with children actively intend to do harm. Good intentions
do not, however, necessarily square with beneficial consequences —
sometimes objectively and, more often, subjectively — for children
and young people.

The major concern of this book is children's perceptions of
personal problems and the help available from adults, particularly
social workers, in dealing with such personal difficulties. Social
work's record of working constructively with children and young
people is not a proud one. The adult world is littered with the never
consulted casualties of the social worker who 'knew best'. It is not a
matter of good or bad intentions, as the reference to Pin Down above
clearly illustrates. It is simply a matter of fact. We believe that the
legacy of practice is another powerful barrier to hearing what children have to say.

It is customary and, sadly, all to easy to recite a litany of social
work's better known failures at this point but as these are not directly our concern, we will pass over them in silence.

Our concern at this point is with the casual, accidental, even
routine abuses committed in the course of social work. For example,

one might allude to the almost infinite capacity of some social workers to misunderstand and misinterpret, with complete confidence, what is being said. Whilst there is ample indirect evidence of this in the accounts given by young people that follow, this tendency to reinterpret the experience of children into terms of reference that an adult social worker will understand is captured exactly in the semi-autobiographical account of her early life by Kaye Gibbons (1990) when she describes an encounter with her social worker:

> He always starts out the same with how important it is for me to relax and say what I feel.
> I do not think I have a problem but he gets paid good money, I am sure, to find out what ails me and cure it.
> So how are you today? he always wants to know.
> Fine I always say back nice and genuine as I can make it because if I tell him the truth like I had rather be digging a ditch than be here today he asks me why I am defensive.
> And then he will not let go of a word but he has to bend and pull and stretch what I said into something he can see on paper and see how it has changed like a miracle into exactly what he wanted me to say.
> Then he will smile all pleased at his self.
> . . .
> Lord I say to him. I hate to tell him he's wrong because you can tell that it took him a long time to make up his ideas. And the worst part is I can see he believes them (Gibbons 1990, p.86ff).

It has been argued that such a propensity is present in all helping encounters. Certainly, the 'unequal relationship' that Martin Davies (1985) described is evidenced with a certain dreadful inevitability in the pages that follow.

Social work practice and families

The power differentials are compounded, however, by a further aspect of the particular construction of childhood that we have identified, namely the invisibility of 'children' against a background of 'families'. For the child to emerge as a client in its own right, distinguished from its family, can be a struggle in itself, although the wisdom of achieving client status remains debatable.

Social work's interest in 'families', rather than children, has been explained in a number of ways. It may be, for example, because social workers are engaged in the soft policing of Donzelot's (1977) brave new world or because of a lasting infatuation with the radical anti-psychiatry of a previous age (Laing and Esterson 1964; Laing 1969) which at least brought people to question the effects of 'family life' and led to the exploration of more child-focused approaches.

A more benign account might trace this concern to the halcyon days of the preventive, Seebohm and radically social working 1970s. At that time there was a justified and increasingly self-evident dissatisfaction with the public care of children. This, coupled with the 'rediscovery' of poverty, contributed to a refocussing of social work effort in the direction of supporting families in the struggle against the effects of 'deprivation'. In an alternately hostile and indifferent world, vitiated by class antagonisms and structural inequalities, the family becomes not only a place of protection but also a source of strength, where the interests of children and adults are united in the face of a common enemy. Parents are prevented from parenting, not by any pathological incapacity but by the stresses of poor housing, poor incomes and poor prospects, conditions endured simultaneously by children and their parents. Helping children in these circumstances means helping parents look after them and helping parents means helping children too.

Such arguments have currency still. Bob Holman, both an academic and a renowned practitioner of 'community social work', has consistently placed the emphasis, in both his writing and his practice, on families as the central focus for social work intervention (see Holman 1981, 1983). He wrote in 1980:

> By failing to tackle social deprivation, by refusing to strengthen effective preventive work and by legislation only for the separation of families, the government . . . casts the parents in the role of those who are not to be helped but are to be punished . . . the fact of living with parents who conceived the child does usually create an affinity and should be the foundation on which socialisation and domestic life is based. The present social system appears to accept this premise for most families but its inequalities inhibit a minority of families from enjoying normal family life (Holman 1980, p.17).

Throughout the 1980s, Holman continued to argue the case for 'putting families first' (see Holman 1988).

Andrews (1980) has also stressed the intrinsic advantages offered by the birth family in providing nurture and protection for children. He appears to be quite satisfied that the assumption that the parent is in the best position to know what is in the best interests of the child is a wholly reasonable one.

The voices of the Family Rights Group, Parents Against Injustice and the National Council for One Parent Families have also risen in support of the pre-eminence of the family. The 'magic of the family' is deeply embedded in the social work literature on child-care where substitute family care is always presented as the preferred option when access to the real thing is prevented (Butler and Owens 1993). Most evidence about the 'family' does indeed suggest that it is the 'best' context for children to grow up, not only in its idealised form, but also even when it is characterised by some degree of tension and dissent.

Broadly, we are in sympathy with the defence of the family that we have outlined here. We would, however, make a number of points which qualify such broad assertions and which bear strongly on the themes of this book.

First, developments in our knowledge and understanding of child abuse, particularly sexual abuse, over recent years ensure that we recognise with renewed clarity the truism that not all families share the same unconditional commitment to family health and harmony as *the* family. That a family can be an oppressive, cruel and hopeless environment for children (Dobash 1977, Dobash and Dobash 1992) should be sufficient to remind us that it is a dangerous assumption to leave entirely undifferentiated the interests of children and their parents.

Secondly, in the writings of those who have been quoted as significant contributors to the defence of the family, the child's own viewpoint is not strongly represented. Although not a necessary consequence of the arguments advanced, the defence of the family does imply that the 'mantel of paternalism' (Fox Harding 1991) may come to obscure the direct expression by children of their interests.

We have no difficulty, however, in accepting, even welcoming, much of what is said in this particular tradition of support for the family. The need for warm, affective and effective relationships between children and adults in the context of their families is apparent in the accounts of young people contained in this book. But so too is their opposite. We warn only against the *assumptions*, deeply embedded in the practice wisdom of social work that the family comes first, that parental interests always coincide with the interests of children and that the adults' construction of family life is the only one to which attention should be paid.

Children and social work theory

Social work's failure to recognise the selfhood of children, while perversely enshrining their 'otherness', may be accounted for also, in part, by the lack of any *consistent or coherent* theoretical base for much of the work undertaken in the field of child care.

Whilst there is no shortage of theories, received wisdom in the field is particularly prone to the whims of what appears to be little more substantial than fashion. Appropriate childrearing practice is the best known case in point.

The advice once given to midwives (and probably social workers if there had been any) which they in turn passed on to the mothers of the thirty-something generation could easily read now like a witness statement drawn up to substantiate allegations of 'significant harm':

> Babies and children, we have been truly told, are all the better for a little 'wholesome neglect'. From the beginning an infant should be trained to spend most of his (*sic*) time lying alone. He gets quite enough handling while being fed and dressed . . . Reserve singing, talking and playing for his (half hour per day) 'playtime'; let 'being amused' be a treat — do not let him expect it always, for then he will get no pleasure from it . . . Do not point things out to him (Frankenburg 1934, p.171).

More recently and more seriously, the Directors of Social Work in Scotland, made the following honest and sobering observation on practice in the field of child protection:

> . . . practitioners . . . are working within a field of evolving knowledge and changing public attitudes and expectations. Often they can find themselves at the forefront of discovery without the support of established knowledge (DSWS 1992, p.5).

An uncharitable gloss on this statement could be 'We are making it up as we go along'.

Without a coherent body of knowledge from our otherwise usually reliable sources in the natural and social sciences, our understanding of practice with children remains confused. And while such fallibility at times causes affront to our professional dignity, its costs are potentially far greater to the lives of children.

Nonetheless, it is better to have some theory and some understanding than none at all. The literature on clients' views of effective helping, depicted prophetically by Howe (1987) as 'The Consumer Reports', is unequivocal in reporting that the clients of social work favour social workers who have a sense of purpose and who are 'straight' about it:

> The need to understand why the worker is involved and what is going on runs through all consumer reports (Howe 1987, p.3).

Furthermore, the relationship too must be right:

> Clients do not like social workers who are cool, detached, career

minded or suggest that they are only doing their job ... Clients
do like workers who show friendliness, homely qualities and
honesty (Howe 1987, p.3).

The children and young people in our study add a particularly
articulate note to the still small voice of *The Client Speaks* (Mayer
and Timms 1970), and one element of their perspective is a confirmation of Howe's contention about the nature of effective social
worker/client relationships.

Despite the burgeoning material on social work theory and practice there remains, however, an absence of many demonstrable suc-
cesses, either in the form or content of practice. Scant regard continues, in many cases, to be paid to the voice of any client, least of all
children who barely emerge from the shadow of their families in the
social work literature. Fashions in our theories of causes and effects
ebb and flow, with the common thread continuing to be an inability
to demonstrate with confidence the efficacy of the knowledge that we
have. With these points in mind, we could do much worse than to
listen to those who have the most up to date knowledge and experience of childhood and the visitations of social work.

Not that listening is sufficient; that which we hear has to be
respected and weighed in the balance with our own knowledge and
experience and allowed, possibly, to form the basis of our future
action. To accept this is to do no more than concur with John Stuart
Mill (see Archard 1993) when he observed that individuals are
usually the best judge of what is in their interests and will act
accordingly. There is little evidence to support the conclusion that
others will know better.

The remainder of this chapter considers the potential of contemporary forms of practice to develop a more child-centred service for
children and young people. We return to the development of practice in Chapter 6 and consider in Chapter 7 how the organisation and
delivery of services might be reconsidered in the light of what children and young people have to say in the intervening chapters.

Social work today

This much is in the past. What about contemporary forms of practice and the framework for social work services provided by the
Children Act 1989? What too of the potential of the consumer satis-
faction society? Will they, together with other recent developments,
not ensure that children's voices are better heard?

There is some hope that the resurrection of 'partnership practice'
from the early grave of radical community development and the

pious injunctions of the Children Act to gather the 'ascertainable wishes and feelings' of almost everyone will give substance to a genuinely child-centred practice. There are grounds for some optimism that a range of constructive partnerships may evolve, of which partnerships with children and young people will be one strand. Buchanan (1994) illustrates some such models of 'good partnership practice', models which we should note have been quietly pioneered over some time in the work of various national children's charities but which are now legitimated within the work of local authorities through the Children Act. But even Buchanan concedes that 'there is still a long way to go' in developing grounded practice which properly squares with the expressed intentions of the Act.

Whether such good intentions will survive the attention of a vicious media, alternating public hostility and indifference around social work with children, draconian cuts in public resources and the precarious future, in whoever's hands, of the welfare state, is not, in our view, a foregone conclusion.

Partnership practice

Partnership practice, like a certain brand of stout was once claimed to be, is good for you. Increasingly these days, the term most commonly used to describe the relationship between the various elements in any social work endeavour is 'partnership'. 'Partnership' is one of the buzz words of the 1990s, a nice sounding term which 'makes us feel good, perhaps even to the extent of being offered as a solution to all child-care difficulties' (Family Rights Group 1991).

Everyone is in partnership: social services departments and health authorities are in partnership around community care; police and community workers in crime reduction initiatives; training and enterprise councils and local business in local labour market development; social workers and families over the provisions of the Children Act; and colleges and service providers over DipSW courses.

At the heart of any discussion about the nature of partnership practice — whatever social work managers may think about it being 'in terms of a jigsaw, some with large pieces, some with small, but all important' (Hutchinson 1994) — lies the question of power. We would suggest that in its everyday sense, the idea of a partnership implies a set of power relations that tend towards equality and mutuality.

However, we have also suggested that there is a power inherent in the role and status of social work and social workers, particularly but not exclusively when operating in a statutory context that tends towards the opposite of what is implied in any dictionary definition of partnership, away from mutuality — towards an imbalance of power in favour of the social worker. Given the relative powerlessness of children generally, the potential for partnership practice with children is far from guaranteed.

The power possessed by the social worker derives from a number of sources, not least a legal mandate and societal expectations (Howe 1987). It derives also from the alleged and usually assumed possession of a body of knowledge and specialist skills — the source of social work's claim to *professional* status (see Johnson 1972).

Part of this set of power relations translates, as it does for many professionals, into a belief that we can determine the best interests of others and indeed, we often feel that we are required to do so. What else are we for? Certainly, we have plenty of scope to do so, especially in our work with children.

It is a very seductive idea that on the basis of status, legal mandate, objectively determined assessments, grounded in practice theory and supported by technical expertise social workers are able to determine which goals and objectives are desirable or attainable in any given social work situation and how the necessary tasks should be allocated, sequenced, concluded and then monitored and evaluated, without any reference to the client, particularly if that client is a child. It is, of course, the use (and misuse) of professional power in this way which has been the focus of academic analysis for many years (see, for example, Kittrie 1971), as well as the basis of recurrent media attacks on the 'untrammelled powers' of social workers.

We came upon a very graphic example of this recently whilst attending a conference on substitute family care in the US. We were presented with what we can only describe as forms of ritualised child abuse. In the name of a variety of particular therapeutic imperatives, children and young people were subjected to sustained and intensive emotional working over, most of this on video tape. Children as young as three or four were left in great sobbing heaps as some off screen voice intoned them to 'really get in touch with their pain' or to 'face the reality of their situation'. The distress of the children did not register at all. Therapist knew best. We objected not only to the exploitation of these children for the purposes of the conference but also to the process itself. We received very short shrift and were accused of being too emotionally involved with the case material — note 'case material', not children. This case material was there to be formed in the image of the therapist. The children would be cured when they conformed to the particular therapeutic regime. What happened en route was unfortunate possibly, but necessary, certainly. (Similar processes have been identified in dealing with young offenders in residential institutions in Britain, in which they are pressed to face up to their problems, when the main problem for many, if not all, is less some personal pathology and more the simple fact of being 'inside' — see Walter 1978.)

We asked what choice young people had in the placement process on these particular fostering schemes in the United States. We were told that they had none. That was the social worker's decision. To share it with the child would be to abandon the responsibility that the social worker carries for the successful resolution of the case. It would be an abandonment of the responsibilities conferred not only by the social work mandate, but which also come, more generally, with adulthood. We return to the question of parental paramountcy across the Atlantic in Chapter 2.

We need to locate the above comments within the context of the continuing uncertainties and insecurities which face social work about its knowledge base, its predictive powers and its capacity to deliver. In such light, it is not unreasonable to argue that we should be willing to admit at least the *possibility* that the users of the services we offer are as likely as we are, to know what is in their interests.

Nothing that we have said, however, should be taken to deny the real power that comes from specialised knowledge, skills, status and legal mandate. That power is real and, as the above examples illustrate, all too easily put into effect. Our point concerns how that power is used. For it may be used *exclusively* to impose definitions or assessments of the problem, or it may be used *inclusively* to empower others, including children. The central message of this book is not only that the latter approach is, predictably, the one *favoured* by children and young people, but it is also the one that is most likely to be *effective* in moving some way towards resolving the problems which are being addressed.

But before we wax too lyrical about partnership practice or its apparently boundless potential, we would want to enter a note of caution. It appears very strange to us that partnership has so few enemies. Taking a stand against partnership is like arguing for sin. One tends to stand out in the crowd!

There does seem to be a remarkable degree of unanimity about the value and importance of partnerships, including amongst those with whom social workers often find themselves in dispute. There is evidence of support from the 'community' end of the liberal left and from the 'rolling back the frontiers of the welfare state' end of the radical right.

We think that this congruence is more apparent than real and deserves some further attention. One can trace a concern with the idea of partnership to a debate extending over at least twenty years. In terms of the liberal left, such concerns go back to the 'patch movement', orchestrated by a variety of agencies keen to promote more grounded inter-agency working which would be more responsive to local communities (see, for example, Williamson and Weatherspoon 1985, Gill and Pickles 1989, Broady and Hedley 1989). One is reminded of the likes of Hadley and McGrath (1980) who advocated the 'patch movement' in social services. Behind the arguments for a 'patch' approach lay a belief in local control and a fear of bureaucracy which, it is alleged, turns citizens into clients.

If one examines the rhetoric of partnership from the radical right which finds expression in the plethora of charters that fall regularly on our doormats, it may appear to start from similar premises but tends towards quite different ends. The thesis here is that as the state has extended its interests more and more deeply into what previously had been considered as the sanctity of the domestic hearth, there has grown, in parallel, considerable administrative discretion in the hands of state functionaries such as social workers — discretion about who receives services and who has access to resources. What has come to be called 'partnership practice', with an enhanced role for the client, provides one way of checking on this discretion, which has increasingly become the object of government and more general public concern.

The Cleveland 'affair' serves as a good example in this respect. Here the contemporary concern was not so much with the abuse of children but with the alleged excesses of the professionals, including the social workers and their apparently limitless power (Butler-Sloss 1988). This is also a theme in the Clyde Report (1992) on the alleged abuse of children in Orkney.

This argument also implies that welfare bureaucracies (Billis 1984) have become very large, distant and inadequate — a particular concern of a very centralist government of the day, concerned with the growing burden of public spending that it finds hard to control.

Thus, right across the political spectrum, similar concerns about the roles, functions and practices of social work have been expressed, seemingly suggesting a unique convergence of radical conservatism and radical liberalism around the idea of *partnership*. But this consensus is more apparent than real.

For us, the interest from the right in ideas of partnership, what one might call the 'charterisation' of public services, is much more of a device for applying, with all its rhetoric of purchaser and provider and the terms of the contract culture, the quantitative techniques of business and commerce to the qualitative areas of social need, health care, income support, law and order, and education. Social problems are not so much resolved by this essentially political and economic argument as redefined to fit the steadily decreasing resources made available. Partnership in this sense means shifting the balance back into the community and away from the state, lowering expectations and disarming any resistance to change in the structure of the welfare state (see McCarthy 1989).

In this sense partnership practice at the macro level may just be the Judas sheep of the radical right. Partnership permits neglect in the community and the 'de-clientisation' of social work with children and families.

We introduce this note of scepticism deliberately because in the social work literature, the idea of partnership practice has been accepted all too uncritically. It is almost universally extolled as valuable and precious in its own right.

We believe that it is possible to identify two strands in the passion with which social workers pursue ideas of partnership; the first sees partnership as something valuable in itself, the second sees it as a necessary component to the success of the social work process. Thus, underlying many arguments for partnership, there is an assumption that it is a right or, if it is not a right, it is at least a good and valuable experience which promotes personal growth and self esteem.

We should be very sceptical of this approach. For everyone else, partnership is valued for what it helps them achieve — for its tangible outcomes, for its *instrumental* value. For the clients of social workers, however, there seems to be an assumption that it is to be valued in terms of how it makes one feel — for its *expressive* value. As such, it has too much in common with so much other social work magic.

We do not wish to completely denigrate the concept of 'partnership', for it does present many opportunities. Equally, however, we do wish to draw attention to the threats presented by the rhetoric of partnership. In particular, we are concerned about the very real potential for partnership practice to revert to no more than another *top down* strategy for intervention. There are real risks that approaches to 'partnership' may be used by professionals to extend their power rather than to share it. All this needs to be recognised and subjected to rigourous debate, for the seductive ring attached to the notion of partnership must not be allowed to conceal the fact that it has both 'conservative' as well as 'radical' possibilities.

The suggestion has in fact already been made, admittedly largely in the United States (see Coit 1978, Arnstein 1972) that partnership is an essentially conservative force which serves to legitimate the existing structure of power relations. Indeed, commonsense would suggest that partnership *can* easily be corrupted precisely because *it is* fundamentally about power sharing. Few people ever give up power willingly, no matter how much they may apparently support ideologies of sharing.

It is more helpful then to conceive of degrees of partnership —

some of which are more cosmetic than others — in order to see that partnership can operate along a continuum determined by the nature of the power relations.

The implication is that, in social work, partnership approaches worthy of the name will require a significant change in the philosophy and practice of many social workers. At the heart of partnership practice lies a set of values that, when scrutinised closely, many would find challenging. The following statement of partnership values, derived from Atherton and Dowling (1989), is but one example:

- Partners trust each other. So they can be open and honest in how they behave to each other. They try to understand rather than to judge.
- Partners respect each other. There is parity of esteem rather than necessarily equality, complimentarity rather than equality where the special skills and knowledge of the worker are made accessible to the client in the way that has been negotiated with the client.
- Partners are working towards the same broad objectives. They are working towards the same end.
- Partners share power. Nobody has a monopoly on it and nobody takes over. That power may never be equal but it should be possible for the balance of power to shift by negotiation and agreement.
- Empowerment of the client can be assisted by ensuring that the views of each partner carry weight and are respected and by sharing information.
- Partners share in decision-making.
- Partners can call each other to account and have rights. Partnership practice does take the issue of accountability seriously and provides for any partner to call for explanations and to challenge what work is going on.

Given what we have said of the scant attention paid to children, in their own right, in past social work practice, how far these principles can be translated into practice in the future remains debatable. The New Jerusalem of partnership practice, particularly with children, still seems a long way off.

We incline to the view that the 'system' will never be so perfect that individuals won't have to be good and would endorse the words of Maureen Stone when she advised social workers recently in a training context:

At the end of the day social workers have to accept that their young clients may make decisions, or choices which appear not

to be in their best interest. This is no different from clients in
other situations . . . The young client may base her/his decision
on factors which the social worker can only guess at. It is
difficult to weigh the cost of one set of actions/outcomes as
against another, when all seems equally dismal and hopeless.
The important thing is that the young person knows that the
child protection service is available and what it does, and has
confidence to approach the social worker for assistance when
they feel able or willing to seek help. It is important to accept
the limits to professional intervention, work within these limits
and accept that we live in an imperfect world (Stone 1993, p.6).

Children, the law and public policy

Although never specifically referred to in the text, 'partnership'
practice is said to be one of the hallmarks of the Children Act 1989.
What other hopes for hearing the voices of children does the Act
offer? Does it empower children?

In considering whether to make a care or supervision order and
in certain other circumstances (CA 1989 S.1(4)), the court is
required to consider, as part of the so-called 'welfare check-list', *the
ascertainable wishes and feelings of the child concerned*' (CA S.1(3)(a);
our emphasis).

This reference to the wishes and feelings of the child and no
reference at all to those of the parents, can be construed as evidence
of the way in which the Children Act in particular, but also the law
more generally, is moving towards an increasingly 'child-centred'
approach to resolving those issues that come before it.

There is a reference to parents further on in the 'welfare check-
list' (CA 1989 S.1(3)(f)). This requires the court to take into account
in reaching its decision, how capable the parents are of meeting the
child's needs. Taken with the above, this would seem to strengthen
the impression that:

> The courts have come to regard parental responsibility as a
> collection of powers and duties which follow from being a
> parent and bringing up a child, rather than as rights which may
> be enforced at law . . . [the term parental responsibility] more
> accurately reflects that the true nature of most parental rights is
> of limited powers to carry out parental duties (DOH 1989, p.9).

In this light, 'parental responsibility', another key concept of the
Act, may be understood as a responsibility *to* children and young
people. It would appear to imply that the rights and interests of
parents are subordinate to their duties towards the child and that, as

the legal position of parents is weakened, so that of the child is strengthened, consistent with the principle of 'welfare para-mountcy'.

This essentially liberal shift is assumed to follow a series of precedents as part of a gradual evolutionary process operating in the courts. Dewer (1992), for example, draws attention to Lord Denning's judgement in 1970 that the legal right of a parent:

> ... is a dwindling right which the courts will hesitate to enforce against the wishes of the child, the older he is. It starts with a right of control and ends with little more than advice (Per Lord Denning in Hewer v. Bryant [1970] 1 QB 357).

This statement was one notable watershed in the changing balance of power between parents and children and has been viewed as a significant precursor of the more widely known judgement by Lord Scarman in the 'Gillick' case, in which the principle was established that:

> parental right yields to the child's right to make his own decisions when he reaches a sufficient understanding and intelligence to be capable of making up his own mind on the matter requiring decision (Per Lord Scarman in Gillick AC 112 at 186).

The 'Gillick' judgement is often cited as the basis of much greater self-determination these days for 'Gillick-competent' children and young people, but it also conceals many other ambiguities left unresolved in the light of the provisions of the Children Act, about which Dewer has considerably more to say (Dewer 1992, pp.105–108).

Nevertheless, in certain other ways too the Children Act itself would appear to strengthen the position of children in relation to decisions taken about them, and not just in the context of court proceedings. For example, a young person aged over 16 may consent to the provision of accommodation for him or herself, irrespective of the wishes of his/her parents (CA 1989 S.20(11)) and the local authority is required to consult the child concerned when any decision is taken about him or her if s/he is 'looked after' by the local authority (CA 1989 S.22(4)). The child also has direct access to the 'representations' procedure that the Act establishes (CA 1989 S.26(3)).

There is surprisingly little contemporary debate on the implied shift in the balance between the rights and duties of parents and the rights and powers of children that may follow from this reading of the Act and it is not clear from what source, if any, either resistance or support might come.

The absence of debate around this issue at the time of the passage of the Act through Parliament is less surprising in that, at that time, the issue was not conceived of in these terms at all. The perceived shift in the balance between the relative legal status of parents and children would have appeared to stand in contradiction to another central theme of the Act, namely the stress that the Act was said to lay on the primacy of the family. We would suggest that any shift in the relative status of parents and children may be an *unintended* consequence of quite different processes at work in this piece of legislation and the political context in which it was framed.

The family, especially the family of origin, is central to the operation of the Act, and much other social policy and to any understanding of the concept of 'parental responsibility' that it implies. (For a fuller discussion of the model of and for the family implied in British social policy, see Van Every 1992.)

The Children Act has been officially described as resting:

> on the belief that children are generally best looked after within the family with both parents playing a full part and without recourse to legal proceedings (DOH 1991b, p.1).

This would appear to give renewed impetus to the primacy of the family as the agent of childhood socialisation.

As Section 17 of the Children Act makes clear, it is now the duty of every local authority towards 'children in need' *'to promote the upbringing of such children by their families'* (CA 1989 S.17(1) our emphasis).

The apparent conservatism of the Act in this regard would seem to jar with the apparent liberalism we have postulated so far but it is wholly consistent, we would argue, with the Conservatism that produced not only this Act but which also froze Child Benefit and changed the Social Security rules to penalize young people living away from home. For, as Freeman (1992) has noted astutely, the apparently broad consensus across the political spectrum which informed the Children Act concealed the considerable *dissent* (reflecting very different ideologies and agendas) which persisted just below the surface.

It is not surprising, therefore, to find commentators now asserting that the formulation of the Children Act connects firmly with what McCarthy (1989) has called the 'new politics of welfare'. In McCarthy's account, these politics, articulated by Norman Fowler as early as 1984, whilst he was government minister responsible for social services, offered the opportunity:

> ... to reduce expenditure and shed responsibilities; ... (they) would strike a curiously populist chord, finely tuned to the Thatcherite emphasis on freedom, self help and responsibility,

which would enable tens of thousands to 'give something back' to their own local communities by participating in social support (McCarthy 1989, p.43).

In this context, the family would have an important role to play. Indeed, ultimately it would be the family that would serve 'in the frontline of care' (*ibid*, p.43).

The importance of the concept of parental responsibility to the Act is to be understood then, not only by reference to how it may affect the relationship of parent to child but also by reference to how it regulates the relationship between parents and the state.

As the boundaries around the legal concept of marriage become less distinct and the social fact of marriage adapts in the face of a variety of competing domestic arrangements, it is *parenthood* that is increasingly being regarded as 'for life':

> [if] the bonds of parenthood are now assuming the degree of indissolubility once accorded to marriage, any significant readjustment in the relationship between the parents themselves and between parents and children is just as deserving of regulation as the dissolution of marriage itself (Eekelaar 1991, p.173).

In establishing the concept of 'parental responsibility' the Children Act can be seen as doing just that. The parental responsibility of married parents can be ended only by death or adoption. Moreover, 'parental responsibility', as defined, can extend and be extended to 'non-marriage' partners including the birth father of the child, where he was not married to the child's mother at the time of the child's birth.

Understood in this sense, the concept of 'parental responsibility' is not to be understood as simply implying that parents are responsible *to* their children, it implies also that parents are responsible *for* their children.

Hence, the state will never assume exclusive parental responsibility for a child. The law will permit the concept of parental responsibility to extend to 'non-marriage' partners. Even where the birth father does not assume parental responsibility, as defined by the Act, his role in maintaining the child financially cannot be escaped, thanks to the provisions of the Child Support Act 1992.

How far local authorities, starved of resources and distracted by the prospect of structural and administrative change, will use the opportunity provided by this conception of 'parental responsibility' as a gatekeeping mechanism, remains to be seen. There is growing evidence that local authorities are substantially more reluctant to go to court and are promoting direct access to legal remedies by parents themselves.

In considering the concept of parental responsibility, one should consider how its operation does imply a shift in relations between parents and children and between parents and the state. The point of balance between these competing tendencies will need to be found in practice. Our point is that any tendency in the Children Act 1989 towards providing opportunities for the child's voice to be heard, is balanced by an equal and opposite tendency to place that voice in the context of the family and we have indicated how such an approach may be disadvantageous to children. The Children Act 1989, despite its positive aspects, offers no guarantee of a more child-centred practice than the rhetoric of 'partnership' does.

Consumerism and citizenship

Cahill has noted that:

> consumerism is a powerful ideology, precisely because it is taken for granted, it is the common sense of our age and all the more powerful for that (Cahill 1994, p.177).

The wider debate concerning the citizen as consumer is beyond our scope but it is an important component of the legal and policy context in which this book has been written. Already, in relation to partnership practice, we have cast doubt on the wider political investment in the changing nature of the delivery of social work services. In its defence of the family and in its 'charterisation' of services, the party of the consumer would like to encourage a belief that it has produced a Bill of Rights for Children and Families in the Children Act 1989, although much remains to be proved.

The all-important question remains: will the child as 'consumer' fare better than the child as 'client' in securing attention to what they have to say?

The influential Short Report noted that:

> The growth in status of the National Association of Young People in Care (NAYPIC), representing what [the Minister] called the 'pure consumer interest in child care', is a welcome opportunity for children to make their views known (Short Report 1984, para.18).

The Report went on, however, to articulate a model of shared care on the basis of the 'considerable sympathy' that the Committee had 'with the advocates of family rights'. The problem with consumerism is identifying the consumer. In our view, it is only rarely the child. The movement towards greater 'consumer participation' in the delivery of personal social services has coincided with the new politics of welfare to mutual rhetorical advantage. There is little sign yet of any practical advantages for children.

Children's world

A measure of our world's imperfections can be sensed if we take even a brief glimpse beyond our own shores to the 'quiet catastrophe' that is befalling children and young people elsewhere: at the 40,000 children who die every day from malnutrition and disease; at the 150 million children who live on with ill health and poor growth or the 100 million 6–11 year olds who do not go to school (UNICEF 1991).

Not that these are problems only for the developing world. The Index of Social Health for Children and Youth in the US, an index of performance in such areas as infant mortality, child poverty, teenage suicide and drug abuse, which runs on a scale of 0 to 100, has fallen from over 70 in the early 1970s to only 36 in 1987. Reported cases of child abuse in New York City have quadrupled from 600,000 to 2,400,000 in ten years, all of which takes no account of, in UNICEF's words, the:

> unknown millions of children [who] are living with loveless affluence, with demoralization, with violence, and with drugs (UNICEF 1991, p.33).

Child abuse can take many forms.

Our attitudes to children, their experience and their knowledge must be seen as part of this 'big picture' because, in the words of Marian Wright Edelman, President of the Children's Defense Fund:

> The inattention to children by our society poses a greater threat to our safety, harmony and productivity than any external enemy (UNICEF 1991 p.31).

Edelman's words are cited in support of developing a 'new ethic' as regards children which implies, for us, giving substance to children's education in the art and science of choice, listening to their construction of their world and attaching value to the meaning they give to it. In a more direct sense than ever was the case before, the fate of all of us rests in our children's hands. As the New York State Governor, Mario Cuomo has observed:

> If compassion were not enough to encourage our attention to the plight of our children, self interest should be (UNICEF 1991, p.31).

Listening to children

All human beings are engaged constantly in giving meaning to their social world. That children may be frustrated in their attempts or even have their interpretations denied says more about the distribution of power and authority in our society than about the validity of children's perspectives.

Children shape their social worlds against a background of almost unremitting failure on the part of adults to shape that world for them at personal, social and even geo-political levels. We do not suggest, naively, that children's perceptions are more or less valid than those of adults. Nor are we advocating an unqualified support for the rhetoric which surrounds individual rights and child liberation.

We could argue for a balance between the exercise of choice and a certain collectivist view of social organisation but to do so would detract from our primary purpose: to listen to what children have to say about the problematic aspects of their lives and the help they want in order to deal with those problems before coming to any conclusions about how to build their perspectives into social work practice.

The purpose of this chapter is to urge the reader to pay close attention to what follows, as free as possible from the cultural predisposition to ignore or devalue what children say. It is not all pleasant reading.

However, before turning to what children and young people have to tell us about their 'worst experiences' and how they deal with them, it is important to set out the context in which we embarked on the research which informs the content and argument of this book. As the NSPCC attempts to forge its developing identity as a 'child-centred' organisation, it decided to establish a research fellowship at the University of Cardiff in order to explore, in the broadest sense, 'the needs of children and young people'. It was agreed that a first task was to make contact with significant numbers of children and young people and 'simply' endeavour to listen to what they had to tell us. The next chapter describes how we went about that task and considers the wider implications, emanating from that research task, for 'social research' with children.

2 Seen but not heard: the research

Introduction

The research on which this book is based was designed to be exploratory. From the outset, it was felt that it would be inappropriate to adopt a rigid methodological approach, since the intention was to forge contact with children and young people from a range of backgrounds in a range of settings. It was anticipated that later interviews would build upon the experience of earlier interviews, using supplementary questions around a core framework of questions put to all children and young people. The research was presented to children and young people as an opportunity for their voice to be heard; if they wished to use their voice, the NSPCC, through the research, was listening. The background to the research has already been briefly described, but the impetus was very much about hearing the voices of children, untrammelled by professional direction or interpretation. Thus, where children sought to pursue a particular line of thought (go off at a tangent?), the researcher listened attentively and waited patiently for an opportunity to resume the main thrust of inquiry. Inevitably, this did at times distract, but not detract, from the dominant themes of the research, but the framework and purpose of the research had been carefully explained in 'warm-up' sessions with children and young people — if they wished to emphasise a particular line of thought, that was their prerogative.

Children and young people themselves decided whether they preferred to be interviewed individually, in pairs or threes, or in groups. As the 'sample' unfolded, greater effort was made to 'target' certain types of young people (in terms of more 'ordinary' and more 'troubled' backgrounds and in terms of age, gender and ethnicity) who were at the time under-represented, in order to secure a balance in the characteristics of respondents across a broad spectrum. It must be emphasised, however, that the research work was essentially a series of individual 'case studies' rather than a statistically representative sample of children and young people. Indeed, some groups of young people, such as those within the care system and those from minority ethnic backgrounds, were quite intentionally *over*represented, since their experiences were considered to be especially important to hear.

The 'building-block' approach was felt to be more likely to generate more in-depth and meaningful data, and to incorporate the views of both children who had experienced fragmented relationships, ill-treatment and social work contact, and those who had not. The objective of the research was, through the use of a flexible, semi-structured set of questions and the allowing of additional 'probing' questions, *to shed light* on young people's feelings and perspectives on issues such as 'worst experiences', anxieties, adult support and professional intervention. Throughout, the research was designed to be sensitive to the needs and wishes of children and young people, since it not only accommodated the method of discussion which they themselves favoured but also put them in control of the tape recorder and the duration of the interview session. It was made quite clear to all children and young people that they could refuse to be interviewed and could terminate an interview at any point. In the event, only one young person actively switched off the tape recorder after ten minutes, said 'I've had enough', and walked out. Three others refused outright and three parents actively refused consent for a child to be interviewed. There were also occasions when 'diversionary' and 'avoidance' strategies were perhaps adopted: young people who, when the researcher arrived, were on the point of going out and those who were not around when the researcher turned up at a prearranged time. But this does not necessarily reflect any antipathy to the research project: it may simply be that co-operation in research is not high on young people's own priorities about their use of time! In contrast, however, other children went out of their way to be part of the research — coming into school when otherwise they would have stayed off sick and rescheduling 'appointments' in children's homes to ensure they were involved. There was, no doubt, an inherent curiosity about the research (a preliminary consent form was always sent out a week or so before a visit — see below), and virtually all young people had heard of the NSPCC and thought it did a good job — usually for babies that got beaten! 'Warm up' sessions, which usually started with what children knew about the NSPCC, tended to increase children's commitment to the research, rather than deterring them from participating.

Table 2.1

Age	Male				Female			
	Total male	Care	Recon. family	Trad. family	Care	Recon. family	Trad. family	Total female
17	1	1	—	—	3	—	—	3
16	2	2	—	—	2	2	—	4
15	9	9	—	—	8	5	1	14
14	22	3	2	17	2	9	14	25
13	17	3	—	14	1	4	16	21
12	8	1	2	5	1	3	7	11
11	13	6	2	5	—	4	4	8
10	12	1	2	9	—	4	5	9
9	5	1	1	3	—	—	4	4
8	1	1	—	—	—	—	—	—
7	—	—	—	—	—	—	—	—
6	—	—	—	—	1	—	—	1
	90	28	9	53	18	31	51	100

The 'sample'

Interviews with children and young people were conducted in nine local authority children's homes, four secondary schools, two junior schools and two youth clubs.

The breakdown of children and young people by age, gender and whether they were living in the care system, 'reconstituted' families or 'traditional' families (with both birth parents) was as shown in Table 2.1.

From this table, we should note that just under a quarter (46) of the children interviewed were in the care system, just under a fifth (40) lived in 'reconstituted' families (usually a birth parent and often a step-parent, but sometimes with grandparents or other relatives), and just over half (104) lived with both birth parents.

Over a third of those children and young people with whom we spoke (74; 34 male, 40 female) were from minority ethnic backgrounds. Fifty-three were of New Commonwealth Asian origin, 16 were of African/Caribbean origin, one was Chinese, one was Vietnamese, and three were of mixed racial origins.

Only one young person did not want the interview to be taped. Forty-seven children and young people were interviewed individually or in pairs (these were primarily children in the care system); the

remainder were interviewed in self-selected groups of between four
and six, although on occasions larger groups were interviewed. The
duration of interviews was very varied. The average time of an
interview was between 30 and 40 minutes: the shortest was ten
minutes and the longest an hour and a half.

The research process

The original intention had been to 'reach' children across Wales and
the West Midlands (as defined by the NSPCC's organisational
boundaries). Relevant contacts within local authorities were identified through an initial communication with the NSPCC's Children's
Services Managers. In order to avoid the risk of 'overload' (and thus
an inability to respond quickly to presenting opportunities for
access), approaches to each local authority's education and social
services departments were staggered. Some authorities felt unable to
co-operate with the research, given competing pressures on time
with regard to new legislative and administrative responsibilities, not
least around the Children Act and recent educational reforms. Other
authorities had recently faced, or were currently facing, critical
media exposure about their alleged treatment of children in the care
system and felt that the subjection of children to yet more 'research'
and 'inquiry' was both intrusive and inappropriate. This immediately narrowed the field for potential contacts on the ground.

With those authorities which were, in principle, receptive to the
idea of the research, it soon became clear that in order to actually
reach children on the ground, it would be necessary to engage in a
time-consuming (and very diplomatic) process of discussion, negotiation and explanation, first with senior managers, then with middle
managers and finally with the managers of specific settings (children's homes, schools and youth clubs). As a result, following consultation with the Child Care Director of the NSPCC in Wales and
the West Midlands, it was decided to target three local authorities
which reflected urban, rural and more cosmopolitan contexts.

Introductory letters sent to senior managers attracted requests
for further clarification of the purposes of the research. (All wanted
copies of the 'interview schedule' which, given the nature of the
research, was not possible to provide, but an outline of the framework of questions was made available.) There were also specific
concerns about issues around possible 'disclosure' of abuse during
interviews and around a white man interviewing young women and
black or New Commonwealth Asian young people on matters of
some sensitivity. Such concerns were allayed mainly because
thought had already been given to these issues by those who had

planned the research: the NSPCC had given an assurance that professional staff would be made available in the event of disclosure; the researchers had made plans for female and/or black colleagues to conduct interviews should this be demanded or required. (Although the researcher asked all children and young people if they minded being interviewed by a white man, none in fact objected.)

Once reassured, senior management identified a contact person within middle management with whom subsequent liaison should take place. These individuals identified a number of settings which would, hopefully, be willing to co-operate with the research. The researchers selected from these lists and contacted specific unit managers.

Consent forms for parents (or, alternatively, those in 'loco parentis') were then sent out to these settings. This explanatory letter-cum-form was circulated through children to parents approximately a week before the day on which it was hoped to interview the children. Gatekeepers, particularly headteachers, often added their own covering letter, stressing the voluntary nature of involvement in the research. The research letter, however, made it clear that unless an active *refusal* by parents was returned, involvement in the research would hinge on the consent of the child. As we have noted already, only three such active refusals were received.

(In the case of children's homes, wherever possible, a pre-visit was arranged — no interviews were conducted, but children present had the opportunity to 'grill' the researcher on what it was all about and then to decide if they wanted to be involved.)

On arrival at each setting to conduct the research interviews, consent forms were checked and young people's willingness to participate was confirmed. There was then usually a 'warm-up' session — about the NSPCC, its desire to listen closely and carefully to the views and opinions of children, and how this was an opportunity for them to contribute to the thinking of the NSPCC in its development of future policy. The 'warm-up' session also presented a forum for the researcher to field 'curiosity' questions from young people. Children and young people then decided how they would like to be interviewed — alone, in pairs or in small groups. In schools and youth clubs, friendship groups were the defining feature of this self-selection; in children's homes, most children elected to be interviewed on their own. Throughout this process, it was constantly reiterated that children and young people were in control of their involvement: they did not have to participate at all, they did not have to be tape-recorded, they could turn the tape-recorder off at any time, and they could leave whenever they wished.

Interviews then flowed for as long as was needed to cover the framework of questions around which the research was based, within the constraints of young people's interest and attention, and sometimes time limits imposed when access to a setting was granted (particularly in schools, when time was sometimes, though not always, rationed to the duration of a lesson). Return visits were sometimes needed to conclude interviews with all willing participants in a particular setting.

Thus, prior to conducting any interviews, there was a six-stage process of exchanging letters, making telephone calls, arranging visits and sending out consent forms.

Effective qualitative research is often a very time-consuming process, which too many methodological accounts of securing access fail to acknowledge sufficiently.

Practical issues

Talking to children and young people does not lend itself to tight structures and defined sequences. Children jump around and researchers have to jump around with them, seizing opportunities to probe and explore issues further. In groups, throwaway remarks and joking around are commonplace; individuals are often — at least initially — shy and nervous, others are cocksure and cheeky. Different skills have to be applied simultaneously: group 'management', individual reassurance, as well as attentiveness and, for a researcher, note-taking (even the sparse notes that are permissible when sessions are being tape-recorded). Balancing these different responsibilities in order to ensure that an interview *develops* and young people do not 'switch off', is rarely an easy task. One has to think systematically and yet spontaneously. A truism about social research is that it takes place in the social world, not in a laboratory. Social researchers have to bend and adapt accordingly and learn to 'read' situations sharply and *very* quickly. Failure to do so risks alienating potential respondents (or, indeed, their 'gatekeepers') and places the research enterprise in jeopardy. A number of issues emerged during this research which are worth recounting.

Bureaucracy

Researchers have to work *with* bureaucracy and fight it — go with the grain and run against it. There was a commendable and apparently genuine concern amongst some senior 'gatekeepers' about research which 'threatened' one more invasion into the lives of children in their charge: they wanted considerable detail and certain guarantees before approval would be granted. In contrast, in other authorities (or departments) there was prevarication and recurrent delays in responding to correspondence and follow-up telephone communication.

Some letters were completely ignored. The simple courtesy of an acknowledgement — even if this prefaced a polite refusal and some simple explanation — would have been preferred. Of course, local authorities are inundated with requests for 'research', from school students doing a project, to postgraduate students writing theses, to professional researchers conducting work on behalf of external sponsors. Their inclination may well be to consign all such requests to a bin and we fully acknowledge the many competing priorities with which senior managers have to juggle. External research is not likely to be high on the list. But it is still a frustration to have constructed a carefully phrased 'official' letter and to simply have no response whatsoever to it.

The research task was to reach young people, *not* to engage in a futile bashing against bureaucratic brick walls. If people at any point in the line did not wish to co-operate, that was their prerogative. All that was required was to say so. What was galling was to be held in limbo, despite follow-up letters in case the first had gone astray, not knowing whether a lack of response was in some way intentional (things were being 'considered') or a product of incompetence and inefficiency. On occasions, one could quite readily understand why some children were so critical of the professional world. And as one officer-in-charge of a children's home put it in frustration:

> those bloody consent forms you sent . . . one social worker
> wanted to know the code number of the memo authorising this
> research. She wouldn't sign it till she knew. It took ages. But
> everything's like that now. Sometimes it's hard to believe that
> this work is meant to be about *children*.

This is the nub of the issue. Delays and requests for clarification when it was clearly about protecting children were fully understood and, indeed, applauded. Similar delays, which appeared to be more a product of someone passing the buck or leaving letters lying in the in-tray, were not. Given the refreshing and speedy co-operation which was furnished to the research by some authorities — showing it was quite possible when the will was there — such action, or inaction, without any explanation, was frustrating in the extreme.

Backchat

A more grounded, substantive, methodological issue around interviewing children and young people relates to dealing with the wit, and sometimes sarcasm, which has been finely tuned by some individuals and is often an integral component of verbal exchange between and amongst groups of young people. Humour is a core ingredient for effective social interaction in the daily lives of children. Researchers, like other professionals, have to *connect* with it in ways which may enhance and develop the achievement of the professional task. Equally, however, in one's attempt to 'deal' with it, there is a risk of completely blowing one's credibility.

In a warm-up session with a class of 11 and 12 year olds in which the headteacher had formally introduced the researcher as 'Dr Williamson' (who happened to be wearing a pair of leather motorcycle boots), the following exchange took place with a boy with obvious 'street cred' (shaved sides of head, two-inch long tie, etc.):

—	Can I ask you a question, sir?
Interviewer:	I've told you, don't call me 'sir'. I'm not a teacher. My name is Howard.
—	Can I ask you a question, Howie?
Interviewer:	Don't push your luck . . .
—	Have you really got a motorbike?
Interviewer:	Yes, an old Honda — a 550 Four . . . do you want to ask me anything else that's more relevant to why I'm here?
—	Yeah, how can you be a 'Dr' when you look like that!!!

At which point half the class collapsed laughing. The researcher had obviously had a run-in with the class joker — and lost. The situation had to be retrieved through a stern 'look, if you're going to mess about, there's not much point my being here', but it was coupled with an acknowledgement of the boy's wicked sense of humour. Had it been solely the former, the odds are that the children would have felt alienated: the individual claiming not to be a teacher was pulling rank like one. Had it been solely the latter, the banter would have persisted and no 'serious' work could have been completed.

The message is, therefore, that such 'ready wit and witty reparti' must not be dictatorially closed down, but it does need to be channelled sideways, otherwise there is a risk that flippant asides will dominate the whole of any subsequent discussion.

Interviewing groups: those who talk too much and those who talk too little

The research was not just about asking the questions. It was also about managing the groups to elicit the views and experiences of *all* participants, not just those who were more eager to talk. This meant creating *space* for the less articulate or less confident to express themselves while endeavouring not to convey any disinterest in what the more vociferous or more articulate were wishing to say. Some interview sessions worked more successfully than others in this regard. The important point is that all participants felt that they had the *opportunity* to air their views — that they had not been 'closed down' by the more dominant members of the group.

'Someone like you'

When asked about the characteristics of adults in whom they might place their trust, it was somewhat embarrassing but also rather flattering that a number of younger children said to the researcher, 'someone like you'. He asked what, more precisely, did they mean by that? Their stock response was to do with someone who smiled a lot, had a sense of humour, maintained a lot of eye contact, did not interrupt, and appeared engaged and interested in what they were saying. For some of them, this contrasted sharply with their ordinary experience of communication with adults (teachers and parents) and confirmed the prevalent view of the desirable characteristics of 'supportive' adults (which we discuss in detail in Chapter 5).

Disclosure

Throughout the process of negotiating access to children and young people in different settings, professional managers expressed concern about strategies for dealing with 'disclosure' (particularly of sexual abuse), which they tended to think 'possible, though unlikely'. The contingency plans made with the NSPCC served to provide them with the necessary reassurance that such possibilities had been seriously considered.

Three individuals (all young women) did disclose events in their lives which they claimed they had not discussed *fully* with anyone else (because of the reservations they had about how those 'others' would respond). Clearly, it would be a breach of confidence to divulge any detail here. However, in two cases, support mechanisms were put in place by the researcher in consultation with two of the young women concerned. In the third case, a younger girl was seeking confirmation that she was not to blame for a situation that had taken place some years before. The fact that the researcher quite independently echoed 'exactly what my mum says' appeared to provide sufficient support; the researcher also provided information about the NSPCC Child Protection helpline, should she want further reinforcement of this message, now or in the future.

Probing

In all the interviews, beyond the common framework of 'open-ended' questions, supplementary 'focused' questions were asked which differed between the interviews. These took three forms:

(i) *Clarification*
Children and young people were often asked to clarify what they meant by a particular comment or viewpoint.

(ii) *Scenarios*
Sometimes young people were unable to grasp an abstract situation and concrete scenarios were provided to help them to think through their feelings and reactions. Commonly, with older young people, a predicament was presented in which they found themselves caught up in a 'drugs' situation which was affecting their schoolwork and from which they wished to extricate themselves, but felt unable to tell either their parents or their teachers — who would they turn to? how would they deal with it?

(iii) *Devil's advocate*
The firmness with which some children and young people expressed their views at times called for a 'devil's advocate' question in order to put them 'on the spot'. For example, the researcher would adopt a parent/teacher/social worker position, presenting counter-arguments or reciprocal criticism.

These are some of the 'grounded' observations about the research process in which we actually engaged. In turn, they throw into relief a whole series of broader, more theoretical issues about conducting social research with children. We believe that they may contribute to a redefining of the debate about appropriate methodological and ethical parameters within which we should seek to listen to children 'on their own turf'.

With hindsight — social research and children

We are acutely aware that children are interviewed for all sorts of evidential, investigative and therapeutic purposes and some of the issues that we raise may have a bearing on interviews of these and other sorts. There is already a literature on the theory and the micro-skills of interviewing children in such contexts (HO/DOH 1992, Stainton-Rogers and Worrel 1993) and we do not attempt to cover this ground. Our concern here is, initially, with interviewing children and young people for the purposes of *social research*.

There is a full supporting literature already in some areas of research on children; for example in respect of participant observation (see Fine and Sandstrom 1988). There is also a full supporting literature on the use of interviews as part of survey approaches to data collection (Marsh 1988, McCracken 1988). But there is noticeably little that addresses qualitative approaches to surveys of children.

Consequently we come to much less prescriptive conclusions than might reasonably be expected. Our observations are offered as part of a continuing commitment to finding ways of hearing what it is that children and young people have to say to us, both individually and collectively. We hope that avenues can be found which will remain both ethically true to a principle of 'listening to children', yet simultaneously able to generate reliable and valid data which will assist more genuinely supportive interventions in children's lives.

'We will ask the questions . . .'

If experience were sufficient qualification, then we would all be experts on children and childhood. Indeed, most of us think we are. We have all been there, seen it and done that. Those of us who work with children for a living, might even claim to have got the T-shirt (though, no doubt, in these commercial times, even the T-shirt would date very quickly)!

As adult professionals and professional adults we just *know* how to talk to children. What issues can there be around interviewing them?

The first and perhaps the most important issue to deal with is precisely this prior assumption of knowledge on the part of the adult. While other forms of ethnocentrism have been more or less successfully challenged over recent years, the strength of adults' belief in their intuitive understanding and knowledge of children has proved remarkably resilient.

Yet the problematic nature of interventions with children and young people is self evident. Our collective attention span, as adults, must be relatively short if we are to judge by how often we seem surprised by what research on children, particularly ethnographic research, has to tell us. Despite there being no study to our knowledge that reports the social world of children to be a relatively simple and comprehensible place, we seem unprepared to acknowledge the maturity and sophistication that children bring to their understanding of the world and their place in it (Coles 1967 and 1986, Denzin 1977). We seem equally unprepared for the realities, sordid or otherwise, of children's lives, whether this be in terms of sexuality (Fine 1981, Martinson 1981), drug use (Adler and Adler 1978), aggression

(Fine 1987) or in terms of social and cultural reproduction (Willis 1978).

We strongly believe that any research exercise must be premised on a preparedness to learn something from people whose views generally do not carry any weight and which takes full account of children's daily experience of dialogue with adults that has too often promised much more than it has delivered (see Chapter 1). The researcher is not necessarily any more an expert on children than he or she might be on nuclear physicists and should not behave or expect to be treated as such. Nor, necessarily is their role one of apologist, advocate or interpreter for children. The conventional research rule of objectivity applies.

The work we conducted is, for the most part, presented as unashamedly one-sided, endeavouring to provide a modest corrective to the adult bias in both theory and practical interpretation which has, too often in the past, penetrated and distorted the worlds of children. Yet taking the comments of children and young people at face value is, of course, hardly unproblematic (Howe 1990) and mediation has to take place without the process of securing the *unmediated* views of children appearing tokenistic, but there are indications that this can be done (Flekkoy 1991). What is critical is that the perspectives obtained are grounded in the genuine social reality of children's lives and in order to achieve this one needs the key to enter their 'social world', which may often be one imbued with secrecy (Varma 1992). In order to *understand* that social world, one needs to adopt a suitably sensitive methodology (on which very little specifically has been written, though see Waksler 1991, also Carrington and Troyna 1988) and to be sure that one is asking the right questions.

In our particular case, as we have already described, the research was designed to be 'illuminative' from the outset — to shed light on the perspectives held by children about, for example, support, neglect and professional intervention. As such, it was important to discuss relevant issues with a broad spectrum of children and young people, some of whom would have had direct experience of certain matters, while others would not. Consequently, some of the 'answers' to the questions posed were based on reality and others on hypothetical situations. Furthermore, some questions were more pertinent to some groups and individuals and, indeed, the research design was premised upon the need to be sufficiently *flexible* to explore, opportunistically, issues raised by children and young people in different contexts and with different experiences. A checklist or tightly-structured questionnaire would have been patently inappropriate.

The research questions we adopted did, however, suggest a

framework for inquiry and discussion with children and young people. They sought to explore their concrete experiences with a specific focus on past or present concerns, a description and assessment of family and professional support already received, what kinds of changes would have made things better, and some speculative observations about future anxieties and desirable support should they materialise.

But given the general level of our understanding of the social world of children, it was important that we grounded our inquiries in the concepts that children themselves employed. We placed a premium on ensuring that in our interviews with children we did not import, uncritically, notions derived from an adult perspective. Nor did we want to draw the framework too tightly. This is more than a plea for the use of age appropriate vocabulary and grammar, although it *is* important to emphasise that apparently unproblematic concepts such as 'safe' or 'bad' do have a generationally different set of meanings and associations for respondent and interviewer.

What we are therefore asserting, as a general point, is that social research practice has to acknowledge the fluid and changing worlds that children inhabit — and that researchers need to consider the structure, content and process of research accordingly.

Opening gambits: creativity and 'style'

Creativity in working with any particular research instrument is also important. We believe that *any* discussion on any issue with children and young people must flow from their experiences. It is hard for them to think the unthinkable. One's framework of questions must be constructed around their experiences, observations and aspirations. One's language, sensitivity (or toughness), and tolerance of tangents must tune in to the individual or group being spoken with. Quite how one copes with the 'dunnos', 'all rights', 'not sures' and 'OKs', *we* dunno — realistically we have to write off some interviews as having provided us with little of substance. No-one can force anyone to make a perceptive (quotable?) comment, although one can — and should — try to get to key issues from a number of different angles. One approach might work, when others have seemingly 'failed'.

But it is hardly surprising that it is often difficult to elicit views and opinions from children and young people — to get them to express *their* views. Most children and young people are not accustomed to being encouraged to articulate their opinions in an open and honest way; they consider them to be unimportant to anyone but themselves, a view often confirmed by the adults around them in their everyday lives.

Trying at least a couple of tacks with the monosyllabic child or young person is to be recommended. Let them discharge their invariable fascination with your tape recorder; just chat about what it can do. Some shout a few obscenities into the microphone, but this often helps to get embarrassment or bravado out of the way and starts to get the ball rolling in a more purposeful manner. If unsuccessful, make a flamboyant appeal to them: 'Come on, I bet you're the first to moan that no-one ever listens to you . . . well, I'm right here ready to listen to anything you have to say'. This usually gets something going, at least for fifteen minutes. We are more in favour of such flamboyance in 'breaking through' to young people than the more measured approaches recommended for 'rapport development' advocated, for example, by the American National Institute of Justice. This suggests that in order to empathise with a nervous child's feelings and indicate the naturalness of such feelings, an interviewer should say something along the lines of:

> I wonder whether it feels scary to talk to a stranger about stuff that is so hard to talk about (National Institute of Justice 1992, p.3).

While we acknowledge below some of the implications of 'stranger danger' for research, we believe that humour and light-heartedness — even when seeking to broach serious issues — seems to be the approach to which most children can best relate. Serious attention to their words and viewpoints comes later.

However, it *is* an indictment of the daily experience of not being taken seriously when *they* want to be taken seriously, created by adults for children, that makes children unfamiliar with the niceties of interview behaviour. That they 'mess about' is a commentary on that experience rather than on anything they may subsequently have to say.

On the other hand, of course, one does encounter individuals who immediately get into full flow and hardly stop for an hour or two. Their observations are often the most powerful and perceptive. Qualitative analysis has always to ensure that such incisive comment is not accorded too much weight, and is properly balanced with the range of more mundane reactions.

Once more, the question of personal style becomes important. We would reiterate that humour and self-effacement are useful personal attributes to take into the interview, though they are rarely mentioned in research methods textbooks. Two further illustrations from our grounded research reinforce the point. One of us told two timid 11-year old Nintendo fanatics that he was a wizard at the game and was promptly handed a joy-stick. Both were past 100 points before the researcher got to 10. They thought it was hilarious that this 'posh git' was so incompetent and suddenly were quite eager to have a chat with him. Similarly, two teenage girls accommodated in the care system divulged that they had felt somewhat press-ganged by the staff of their children's home into co-operating with a research interview but, after it had finished and they had gone out for the evening, the officer-in-charge said to the researcher, 'you can come again, they think you're a good laugh'. And they had provided by far the best interview up to that point in the research.

We are not suggesting, however, that you attempt to 'go native'. It is doubtful whether you could produce a convincing performance either in terms of dress, pose or vocabulary. Age inevitably, unavoidably, creates its barriers and divisions and no child or young person wants to talk to any adult who is patently falsely projecting too youthful an image or persona or self-consciously letting fly with contemporary street *argot*. It is important also, though, to avoid any 'distance' that can legitimately be avoided — to acknowledge that you are not always the expert and be prepared to let the assumption of competence, proficiency and influence slip a little with your dignity.

Personal style can affect the actual organisation of the interview process which in turn affects the nature of the interview itself. In real settings where contact was made with real young people (schools, youth clubs and children's homes), staff breathed an obvious sigh of relief when the interviewer did not turn up with clipboard and questionnaire, expecting children or young people to be ushered in at fifteen minute intervals. For some, that had been a genuine previous experience of 'researchers'. Some were clearly cautious about us, having received 'yet another bloody memo' to inform them that 'Dr Williamson, who is doing research for the NSPCC' would be getting in touch.

In relation to the front-line 'gatekeeping' professionals through whom we sought access to young people (teachers, youth workers and residential social workers), we stressed our willingness to be flexible. We made it clear that we knew that children and young people are unpredictable. 'Appointments' would be broken. Young people would discover more pressing 'agendas', like going shopping or watching cartoons. Some kids would mess around. Some interviews would be hopeless (and, of course, some would be brilliant). In our negotiations with these gatekeeping professionals the fact that we understood the context of *their* work, that their workplaces were *not* a laboratory for us to conduct our 'research', put them at ease. And this proved critical in winning their support.

Authority, responsibility and disclosure

Behind the projection of personal style, however, lies the issue of
authority. Whereas the task of the ethnographer is to establish the
trust (Fine and Sandstrom 1988) of the group being studied, the task
of the interviewer may be perceived as a lesser one of establishing
rapport. In reality, this is no more than a matter of degree and the
larger issue is the one of authority (see Reid 1986). Adults are both
seen to and in fact do occupy roles of 'direct formal authority' (Fine
and Sandstrom 1988) over child informants in a way that they do not
over adult informants, except in the most exceptional circumstances
(Goffman 1961).

We have indicated already how the self-imputed authority of the
interviewer might impede the interview process and outcome but the
full force of the issue arises with the emergence, through the interview, of 'guilty' or other uncomfortable knowledge. If one comes to
learn during the course of an interview of a continuing situation that
might be described as abusive or hear of high risk behaviour or
criminal intent, how is one to respond?

In their taxonomy of roles for ethnographic researchers, who
have time on their side, Fine and Sandstrom (1988) indicate that the
assumption of the 'least-adult role' (Mandell 1988), may have some
advantages over their own preferred role as 'friend to one's subjects'.
Yet, ultimately, theirs is a situational and a personal morality.
Where the risk is physical and immediate, Fine and Sandstrom are
unequivocal:

> Children can place themselves in danger. In that event, an adult
> participant observer has a moral obligation to assist them in a
> way that is 'protective' . . . (Fine and Sandstrom 1988, p.27).

Yet their general conclusion allows considerably more scope for
manoeuvre:

> [It has been] suggested that on occasion it may be necessary to
> subordinate the self to the role [of researcher] in the interest of
> research, but, even so, in dealing with children there will be
> occasions when one's authority should be used to enforce moral
> imperatives of the self (*ibid*, p.28).

Many years ago one of us had direct experience of this problematic, during participant observation research with young offenders:

> One of my key informants was a boy who not only spread my
> reputation for 'keeping my mouth shut', but also spent much of

his time in my house. He was a most adept burglar, although he had been caught and convicted a number of times and had been sent to Detention Centre at the earliest possible age — fourteen. He was one of my closest contacts, and was intelligent and articulate; in contrast to my interaction with many others (when serious conversation would dry up within ten minutes), we spent a great deal of time discussing not only my research interests but also a variety of contemporary issues, particularly race, marriage and homosexuality! Whenever he started talking about 'housework' (his euphemism for burglary) I usually warned him of the possible practical consequences — Borstal — and left it at that. I rarely passed any moral judgment on his behaviour.

One evening he came round with the blunt introduction: 'I'm just off to do a job, but there's time for a cup of tea, alright?'. We had a cup of tea and he repeatedly stressed that he was about to go and 'do a job'. In turn I said 'that's up to you'. He left, saying that he was going home for something first. I pondered over his uncharacteristic behaviour for a few minutes, coming to the conclusion that he might well be testing me out to see how concerned I was for him. I certainly was concerned at a personal level. I had no doubt that he was sincere about going to do a job. I made a spontaneous decision and rushed over to his house, catching him as he was about to leave . . . (Williamson 1981, p.531).

The researcher spent the entire evening with him, playing cards and then walking around the streets. He was irritated that the presence of the researcher was 'cramping his style', but finally — with some embarrassment — expressed 'thanks' for (temporarily) keeping him out of trouble. The account of this episode continued:

I know that in personal terms I made the right decision, but remain unsure whether it was the correct course of action on a methodological level. But I do believe this example provides an incisive illustration of the kinds of dilemmas which are ever-present (though usually just below the surface) in research which involves participant observation (Williamson 1981, p.532).

The cultural norm clearly holds that a child's right to privacy and self-determination is not an absolute but a *developing* one, as is their legal right to independent action. It is not at all clear quite how the social researcher should relate to this. While we do not invite the comparison, there are parallels to be drawn to alternative, 'social action' responses such as 'Knuckle Sandwich' and 'The Paint House' (Robins and Cohen 1978, McGuire and Daniel 1972) which stressed that interviewers need to become part of the action (or at least, part of the furniture) before young people are likely to respond honestly.

In the course of the research on which this book is based, we certainly found that young people do identify uncalled for interventions, as well as the clumsy and precipitate handling of disclosure (breaches of confidence?) as particularly harmful. On the other hand, they do find useful the opportunity to talk over problems with the security of *complete* confidentiality — meaning that further action will *only* be taken with the full consent and knowledge of the child.

However, on the basis of a short research interview, as opposed to the relatively long acquaintance that, for example, a participant observer might have with a child, there is very little to guide making a judgement either of the degree of 'risk' or the relative competence of the young person in any given situation.

For, despite the inevitable difficulty of making reasoned situational judgements and the obvious dangers of employing a purely personal morality, there is little professional guidance for the interviewer seeking to conduct social research on children and young people around issues of harm, risk or neglect. The Code of Ethics of the British Sociological Association, for example, makes no explicit mention of children whatsoever.

It is by no means clear to us that any extension or amendment to the BSA Code would be possible given that there seems to be little consensus from which such changes could be developed. That this is an open question is made clear by reference to the situation in the United States. There, building on Federal Regulations (45 Code of Federal Regulations (CFR) 46), subsumed by the National Institutes for Health in 1974, the Department of Health and Human Services adopted additional regulations in 1983 (48 Fed. Reg. 9814, 1983) governing research involving children. Essentially these Regulations permit research on children, only provided that, *inter alia*, parents consent.

Although there is provision under a 1981 revision of the original Regulations to waive parental consent, this is subject to State Law which generally preserves the superior legal and juridical status of parents, a position that most Europeans would now find unacceptable.

Parental paramountcy is implied in Stanley and Sieber's recent commentary on the Regulations. Here, sympathy is extended to the researcher, who:

> . . . does not enjoy spending precious research resources and
> enduring the attrition of a carefully selected sample in the

process of obtaining consent, especially from parents who may disrespect or misunderstand science (Stanley and Sieber 1992, p.4).

But in order to recognise how much weight such considerations should carry:

> Researchers need only ask themselves what wrath they would unleash on a stranger who tried to usurp their parental role ... (ibid, p.4).

How far we are prepared to proceed in securing the views of children and young people without parental consent and with what degree of guaranteed confidentiality, remain acute problems for the intending interviewer, as the issue of adult authority in relation to children remains unresolved. We have already recounted that our approach was, through 'gatekeepers', to seek parental consent to their children being interviewed.

There are two core problematics in this approach. First, by using the children themselves as the carriers of the letters to parents, how can we be sure that parents in fact saw them? Our only confidence on this question stems from the fact that there was no subsequent comeback from irate or concerned parents after the research interviews had taken place, but this still sidesteps the issue of those parents who show little interest in what their child has been doing at school or at the youth club. (In the case of children looked after by the local authority, consent was sought through either parents or social workers or, in some cases, both.)

Secondly, we remain unsure what we would have done had a potential respondent sought to override an active refusal by a parent. There was only one glimpse of this possible problem when the broad purpose of the research was being outlined in a 'warm-up' ten minutes to a class of nine- and ten-year olds. The one child whose parents had actively refused to allow their participation looked positively disappointed that they could not take part, but the class teacher made it absolutely clear that their parents' decision could not be overturned. Unlike the USA, we do not necessarily have the paramountcy of parental consent enshrined in any code of conduct, but once the strategic decision is made to consult parents it would clearly be ethically unsound to run roughshod over parental refusal, *even if the child still expressed a wish to participate.* An alternative approach which by-passed parents and simply consulted with children would, however, be unlikely to be supported by the institutional 'gatekeepers' on which we, and many other researchers, are dependent for access to children.

'Gatekeepers'

The presence of an adult whose role in relation to authority remains unclear (the researcher) certainly complicates the lives of those adults who do have authority over and responsibility for children (teachers, youth workers, social workers) and for this reason the importance of securing the support of gatekeepers cannot be overstated. The abiding lesson from our research is that one must anticipate substantial difficulties in securing access to groups or to individual children when engaging in qualitative approaches to surveys of young people on even as modest a scale as ours. In our case, the obstacles were formidable.

In part these could be attributed to the defensiveness of various 'gatekeepers' to children whenever concepts of 'harm' and 'risk' are mentioned. It is invariably equated immediately with 'abuse' and the warning bells this concept signals — partly from a desire to protect children from further unwanted intrusion, but also because these 'gatekeepers' are currently in a 'no win' situation. They have already been on the receiving end of critical political and media responses whatever forms their professional interventions have taken.

In endeavouring to secure access to children and young people in institutional settings in the past we have always favoured, from the outset, making informal contact on the ground to ensure that, having negotiated the formal channels at higher levels in organisational bureaucracies, the front-line gatekeepers to children and young people would provide the necessary support. This does, however, pre-suppose that one knows the settings one wishes to cover in advance. In this research we did not. Access routes were, therefore, very much a 'top down' process, starting with a general letter to senior officers outlining the broad thrust and purpose of the work and inviting further exploration of the issues.

We have noted already that some authorities or departments refused point blank to assist with the research, invariably on the grounds of the current formal pressures they were under, such as visits from the Social Services Inspectorate, the new requirements under the Children Act 1989, and numerous 'reforms' in educational policy and practice.

For example, one response from a local authority social services department read as follows:

> I have [now] had the opportunity to consider further your
> proposals. Unfortunately I do not feel that I am able at this
> point in time to contribute to your research project. Any
> involvement would require a considerable amount of
> preparation and support of individual children, and I am afraid

that I cannot prioritise it at this point in time given the considerable pressures already upon my staff.

I am sorry that we are not in a position to assist you.

Others quite rightly raised a number of key questions to which they required satisfactory answers before deciding to proceed further — these were concerned with matters such as wider professional support, confidentiality, parental consent and feedback. Despite the diligence and general supportiveness on the part of these senior gatekeepers, the research was dogged by numerous delays. Requests for research co-operation are clearly not considered to be much of a priority in social services and education departments perhaps, as we have already suggested, because they are inundated with pleas to help with 'research' from *individuals* undertaking school and college projects, as well as bona fide research *institutions*. And although we responded to *their* responses almost by return of post, we then often had to wait three or four weeks for the next communication.

We recall the feeling of elation when — after four months of painstaking negotiation — one of us finally 'hit the ground' in one authority, paying an informal visit to a children's home to deliver parental consent forms and actually meet with some of the young people who were likely to be participants in the research!

The broader message is, therefore, that establishing the *framework* within which effective social research with children can be conducted can be a time-consuming process, sometimes leading down blind alleys which, sooner or later, it is wiser to abandon. Without the benefit of hindsight, however, it is often difficult to know which access routes are *temporarily* obstructed by professional or bureaucratic prevarication and which have become dead-ends. What is clear, either way, is that reaching children within 'safe' institutional settings requires patience and acceptance of numerous delays.

Such problems do not diminish even if one intends to secure access to young people in less formally 'gate-kept' situations. An important and probably very necessary component of the contemporary construction of appropriate relations between children and adults is founded on the idea of 'stranger danger'. With some justification, children (and, indeed, adults) view with suspicion, if not hostility, approaches to engage in dialogue with adults whom they do not know personally (see Horan quoted in Fine and Sandstrom 1988).

Fortunately, given our 'snowballing' approach to constructing a 'sample' (based primarily on age, gender, ethnicity and type of 'setting') we did not have to address the implications these issues could have for sample attrition. We simply had to keep 'plugging away' in order to build up the necessary numbers. For those with more rigid sampling strategies, our rather dispiriting account of the potential for sample attrition, resulting from numerous institutional and professional obstacles, needs to be considered with great care.

Sample size might further be affected at the point at which young people themselves give informed consent to the interview process. This issue has been more extensively reviewed in the literature on ethnographic accounts of the social world of children. All we would wish to say here is that most children and young people are often only too eager to talk — *provided they believe that the interviewer is genuinely concerned to hear their stories and provided they are confident that things will not go any further unless they agree to it.* Inspiring the trust and confidence of children within a limited time-frame does, of course, pose problems and we have already alluded to some of the methods by which this may be achieved. The important message here, however, is that nothing can ever be guaranteed. The effective 'throwaway' line with one child or group of children which secures the possibility of moving forward may be equally counter-productive with another individual or group. Children and young people make quick judgements as to whether an individual (researcher or otherwise) is 'all right' or a 'dickhead', and once such judgements have been made it is difficult to alter them without the unavailable luxury of time.

What became apparent from the comments of the children we interviewed was that they assessed adults (parents, relatives, professionals, researchers) initially in terms of what can only be described as 'maverick' qualities, of which humour was a central part. Being a 'good laugh' was a critical attribute. This is completely understandable when we reflect that young people's lives are routinely about backchat, sharp remarks and flippant asides, often all the more so amongst those experiencing difficult childhoods. What young people sought from adults was some serious listening inside a funny shell — and researchers seeking in-depth views and information were no exception. Whether or not having a certain type of hairstyle, wearing particular types of clothing or being knowledgeable about football or pop music was particularly significant is debatable, but there is little doubt that such factors may, on occasions, have the potential to 'swing' things in the researcher's favour. But such self-presentation has to be carefully managed: someone perceived as a 'biker' is unlikely to go down well with the aspiring skinhead, unless the researcher can somehow make an appropriate joke about it. 'Chameleon'-like self-presentation, open to flexible interpretation, is an important feature of striking up an immediate, *personalised*, rapport with children and young people. It is not something on which social research textbooks tend to dwell. Yet it has a critical bearing on effective research relationships where the primary *raison d'etre* is to allow children to feel comfortable in talking freely with a 'strange' adult. Furthermore, this 'management of self', as we have noted, therefore may well demand some element of self-parody, for the key issue is about 'reading' and then forging the necessary links with the child's personal and cultural interests.

Finally, one issue which was always high on the agenda of senior professional gatekeepers was ensuring provision could be made for children to be interviewed by researchers of the same gender or ethnicity, if they so wished. Contingency arrangements were in fact made on this front, but they were not required. All the research interviews were conducted by a white man. Female and black or Asian children and young people were, as we have mentioned already, always asked how they felt about this. They were quite unanimous in their response: they would make up their own minds and the issue *for them* was whether or not the researcher seemed able to grasp the circumstances and perspectives they were describing. If not, they would exercise their prerogative to abandon the interview — and not one did. We believe that although the question is one which at all times merits careful handling, the answer is not as self-evident as many in the professional worlds of social work and education would contend.

Conclusions

We live in a policy climate in which extraordinary circumstances too often dictate the form of 'ordinary' interventions. The determination of government to re-establish more punitive (and ineffective) juvenile justice measures as a result of a small number of tragic, but completely atypical although media-worthy, events is but one example. We fully concede that interventions with children must acknowledge and take heed of the situation and circumstances of a small number of highly disturbed and damaged young people. This applies to research activity as much as to any social work intervention. However, we would also wish to argue forcefully that this minority should not determine the approach taken with most children and young people, whose anxieties and needs are also important and who can — given the right kinds of research intervention — express them articulately and confidently. We risk getting bogged down in the specific issues affecting the most troubled children to the detriment of the general issues which concern the larger body of 'ordinary kids'.

The more 'theoretical' observations we have proffered are designed to outline some of the factors which we believe should inform an effective approach to eliciting the views of that majority. The occasional flippant remarks are not intended as such, for they convey a serious message about how we can make the necessary connections with children and young people. It is time that re-searchers re-evaluated their strategies for talking to children so that they suspend some of the methodological niceties which can be trawled from the textbooks and substitute them with a range of personal sensitivities which are most likely to secure credibility with those whose views they are seeking to reflect, analyse and represent. Listen, and be prepared to learn. That is what we endeavoured to do.

We remain the first to concede that our research was confronted with uncertainties, concerning both securing access to young people and obtaining relevant substantive data. Despite innumerable and sometimes frustrating delays around the former, the latter was ulti-mately achieved.

The analysis of qualitative data is a complex task which does not lend itself to coding boxes and dispensing frequencies and cross-tabulations. It requires a careful, painstaking, sifting of broad themes from what is inevitably always incomplete and varied infor-mation derived from the different biographies and perspectives of the individuals concerned.

Perhaps the most illuminating finding from our work is the cau-tion with which a majority of children and young people relate to the adult, and especially the professional, world — a finding which needs to serve as the basis for reflection and consideration of how that world can re-connect with the experiences and anxieties of the children whose care and support is their responsibility. 'Child-centred' research has its part to play in that process.

It is this theme which unfolds powerfully in the ensuing chapters and which forms the basis of our consideration of the implications for future social work policy and practice.

3 Children talking

Introduction

In order to work effectively with anyone in a social work or other 'helping' context, there needs to be some determination of what the problem is that needs to be addressed. That determination, one hopes, is a negotiated one, in that not only may perceptions of causation vary between the parties to the process, so too might ideas as to what the priorities in any plan of action should be. We have suggested that the balance of power in social work relationships, especially in social work relationships with children and young people, is strongly in the social worker's favour. It is conceivable therefore (and we would argue that it is, in fact, very likely) that children and young people's perceptions of what the problems are and what needs to be done about them will vary substantially from what the adults might judge to be the case, but that it will be the adult's perceptions and priorities which will come to dominate the course of subsequent events.

This and the next two chapters begin to explore what the children and young people to whom we spoke understood as the 'worst experiences' of their lives and how they would want adults to respond to them and their circumstances.

Before we proceed to explore these accounts, it is necessary to make a further few, brief observations. We must make it clear that we did not talk to young people about child abuse. Just as we have argued that childhood is a social construction, essentially one devised by adults with little reference to the actual experiences of children, so too might we argue that child abuse is also a social construction derived from the concerns and perceptions of adults rather than children (see Rogers *et al.* 1989). We shall content ourselves, at this point however, with some semantic and conceptual distinctions. First, we would point out that not all hurt experienced by children and young people is the consequence of what is commonly implied by the term 'child abuse'. The proverbial misfortune with the proverbial bus is certainly harmful but, conventionally, wholly accidental. The essential component required to make an event abusive would seem to us to require either intent to do harm, recklessness on the part of the perpetrator or involve some deluded state concerning the effects of certain actions on the child. The absence of any or all of these components does not necessarily diminish the hurt felt by children in a given set of circumstances. The bus, for example, would still hurt whether one stumbled or was pushed. That we, as adults, respond to certain forms of harm to children (such as child abuse) more readily than we respond to other forms of harm to children is an issue we shall consider further below. Our point here is that in reading the following wholly subjective accounts of painful personal experiences, we would urge that the accounts be considered in their own right and not dismissed or devalued because they do not conform to some existing classification of child abuse.

Similarly, we would urge that these accounts should not be read through a filter of preconceptions concerning child protection, a term which adults use to describe a whole range of preventive as well as reactive strategies for responding to child abuse. We believe that the accounts that young people provide of adult responses to personal problems and painful experiences, including abuse, challenge some accepted notions of what protects children and how that protection is achieved. They should not be discounted simply because they would not find a place near the top of a child protection social worker's current caseload.

Finally, we do not intend that these accounts of worst experiences, real and potential, should be judged against the 1989 Children Act's criterion of 'significant harm'. Although the Act offers a very flexible definition of harm and commentaries have made it clear that the significance of the harm should be considered in relation to the child concerned (Family Law 1994), we understand that in practice, 'significant harm' is rarely to be distinguished from 'life threatening'. We argue for a more generous interpretation than that.

Children talking

After preliminary introductions allowing children and young people to 'settle' into the interview (during which they conveyed some 'positive' things about themselves in terms of, for example, musical interests, hobbies and favourite things and provided a potted 'life history'), they were asked about their worst experiences to date in their lives. Many responses were, in some senses, predictable; some were not. In one or two exceptional cases, apparently 'worst' experiences emerged in accounts of life histories. Only when these were reiterated in order to confirm them as worst experiences did it transpire that in fact, despite their severity on most official continua of abuse and vulnerability, they were not considered so from the point of view of the young people concerned. The most salient example is of the 16-year old young woman who had been raped by her step-brother at the age of 11:

> *Interviewer:* So presumably being raped was the worst thing
> that has ever happened to you?
> —   It was bad, but not the worst. The worst was when
> my step-brother held me still — he used to get
> extra pocket money off my dad for helping him hit
> me — and then my dad broke all my fingers, one
> by one . . .

This reveals that the objective horror of particular experiences may conceal *less* objectively awful events which have a more lasting impact in the subjective memories of young people.

However, 'worst' experiences *usually* lay along a predictable continuum so that, for example, parental violence was, more often than not, the culmination of earlier, routine parental friction. Conversely, if arguments between parents were presented as the worst experience, it was unlikely that actual physical violence had been witnessed or experienced. Thus those whose 'worst' experiences were located around disputes with siblings over access to computer games, or to do with the pressures of homework, had had — at least in conventional professional judgement — relatively untroubled childhoods. That is not to say that the children themselves experienced such episodes in relatively unproblematic terms.

Clearly, children in the care system had often had experiences which were quite unimaginable amongst children in more conventional and harmonious family contexts. Yet the experiences of this latter group should not be immediately discounted for, certainly in terms of bullying and name-calling at school, they were often the young people least able to 'handle' it. For them, therefore, such experiences took on a greater negative meaning than for those who were already 'hardened' to wider worldly realities through the experience of more traumatic events in their lives.

Three young people were adamant that they did not wish to expand upon a general observation that their worst experiences had been 'personal' or 'family' problems. This desire not to divulge anything further was, of course, respected, although one would probably be correct in speculating that they had had deeply troubling and quite possibly abusing experiences. Another young person initially adopted a similar stance, though later she interjected with 'oh, I might as well tell you — my dad killed my mum'. This unusual circumstance (though see Hendricks *et al.* 1993) had obviously been traumatic enough for a nine-year old girl, but it then transpired that the real trauma had been the lack of information or explanation about these circumstances, which had led to her being admitted to care:

> I never saw my mum in hospital after my dad attacked her. I didn't go to the funeral. I don't even know now where her grave is. Nobody told me anything, probably because they thought I was too young. But nobody even tried. And I can't ask now 'cos all the staff who were here then have moved on. But that was actually worse than my mum actually dying . . . (girl, 17).

Other 'associated traumas' around apparently 'worst experiences' will be discussed in conclusion to this chapter.

Only five young people found it impossible to describe any kind of bad experience. One was a white girl, the others were four 12/13 year old Asian young women who asserted forcefully that:

> Our life is all around our families, going to school and going to the Mosque. That's good. It protects us — keeps us safe . . .

A small number (15) of young people of secondary school age associated their worst experiences with the pressures of school work, especially *homework*, summarised in the comment 'always panicking, parents always moaning, teachers always bollocking — you can't get away from it' (boy, 14). An even smaller number (five) of younger children located their worst experiences around *squabbles with siblings*, particularly in relation to disputes over access to home computer games. And a similar number identified what they saw as unreasonable control and restriction within the home as their worst experiences, usually concerning being kept in when they wanted to go out or being expected to be in at a time when others in their peer group were still permitted to be out. Such experiences might well be presumed to be commonplace and hardly a matter for concern. Yet it is important to retain them in mind both because, at one level, they represent the 'worst experiences' perceived by a 'lucky few' but, at another level, they convey the point that even apparently fleeting, apparently 'ordinary' childhood experiences can be perceived as problematic for those who have been fortunate enough not to have experienced anything worse.

However, the most significant 'worst experiences' were, for those living in relatively untroubled family contexts, located within *school* and, for those with more troubled family backgrounds, located around *family* tensions, violence and separation.

Bullying and name-calling

No fewer than 65 children and young people said that their worst
experiences had been physical or verbal bullying at school — experiences which, for many, were still continuing to trouble them,
although others had developed methods of avoiding or counteracting
it:

> When I first went to secondary school I got binned and bushed
> loads of times. It was terrifying. I was only small so I was
> always the one they picked on. Someone's got to be the victim,
> I suppose. At first, bullying really worries you. You think it will
> never stop. But things get better as you move up the school.
> People pick on other kids instead (boy, 14).

> Older kids are always pushing me around, piss-taking, laughing
> at me. I don't know why. I haven't done anything to them.
> Every day when I have to go to school, I get frightened that
> they're going to pick on me again today. I just try and hide and
> hope they don't see me (boy, 12).

> The bullying at school can be really nasty. Sometimes, just
> before break time, I start to shake in class because I'm so scared
> about going outside (girl, 13).

> The worst thing is at school when you go out into the
> playground. The older kids come over and take your bag off
> you and chuck it around, or nick your hat and won't let you
> have it back. You get really upset, 'cos they're all laughing at
> you and you look stupid in front of your mates (boy, 12).

> Because I'm quite good at school, I get picked on by the other
> girls who call me a 'snob' and poke and push me around.
> Sometimes I don't really care, but I must admit I do find it hard
> to fit in and that gets to me sometimes (girl, 14).

Bullying was perceived as an almost 'natural' part of school life, but
it was nonetheless 'terrifying' for those who experienced the brunt of
it. Accounts of bullying episodes spanned the spectrum described by
Tattum, including physical and extortion bullying (Tattum and
Lane 1988, Tattum 1993, see also Fontaine 1991). The really bad
thing about such experiences, according to these children and young
people, was that to admit your terror would almost certainly make
things worse. The best you could do was to put up with it and hope
that sooner rather than later the bullies would move on to pick on
someone else (a view expressed by a 13-year old girl).

Despite the old saying that 'sticks and stones may break my
bones but names can never hurt me', more young people described

name-calling as their worst experience than physical bullying. Fat, thin, tall, short, blond(e), dark — all were vulnerable to verbal ridicule, the more so if they wore glasses, had big ears or had a specific visible ailment or disability, such as eczema or alopecia. Even during the research interviews, children were clearly upset when discussing being referred to as 'matchstick man', 'Dumbo', 'hairy nose' or 'veggie breath': 'it may be a bit of fun to them, but it's not to us' (boy, 11).

Three 12-year old girls recounted the frequency with which they were verbally targeted, culminating in one observing:

> You do get used to it, 'cos it happens to everyone. You just ignore it. Otherwise they pick on you even more. But just because you ignore it doesn't mean that it doesn't get to you (girl, 12).

Children who wore glasses were always vulnerable to verbal ridicule as, of course, they have always been in the past:

> What gets to me most is being called four eyes. I hate it, really hate it. I can't help it if I have to wear glasses. Sometimes I just want to take them off, even if I can't see without them. Maybe it's better not to be able to see than to be called names all the time (boy, 11).

Name-calling was not, however, always directed at the individual's personal characteristics but, where there was knowledge of their wider circumstances, at vulnerabilities which could be exploited there. One 17-year old young man in care reflected on this issue:

> I just couldn't get on with my mum. There were always arguments. I couldn't do anything to please her. My dad had left when I was three. I can't really remember that. Mum was poor — I don't know how she got by. The worst thing was the comments I got at school. Other kids used to say 'your mum's a dog'. And I used to say to myself, 'I don't really care what they say, I can handle it'. But it wasn't true. I was just a vulnerable 10-year old, they knew it and those comments hit *deep*.

The *depth* to which name-calling can affect young people should never be underestimated, nor should its persistence over time:

> Name-calling grinds away. What's supposed to happen is you ignore them and its supposed to wear off, but it never wears off (boy, 10).

Family arguments, violence and abuse

For other children and young people, negative school experiences paled in significance in the light of what had taken place in and around the 'family'. Too often, the perceived or desired security of a family context had been violated, with children usually as hapless and helpless witnesses and sometimes as the targets of parental violence and abuse. These worst experiences were graphically illustrated in the observations made by children and young people.

Seventeen children and young people identified *family arguments* as their worst experiences. These were invariably, though not exclusively, between parents; occasionally grandparents, uncles, aunts and siblings were also involved:

> I can hear my parents arguing when I'm lying in bed at night. Sometimes they're arguing about me. I can't sleep and I can't stop worrying. Quite often I'm afraid to go down in the morning (girl, 14).

> The worst thing is the arguments between my mum and her new boyfriend. He's horrible. He's nasty — he's always teasing me. I talk to my nan and grandad and then they have arguments with my mum. My dad says 'don't worry about it', but it's horrible. It goes on all the time (girl, 10).

Aggressive verbal exchanges often spill over into more physical confrontations within the family. Twenty-seven children and young people discussed *family violence* as their worst experiences — most often between birth parents, or a birth parent and step-parent. Frequently, physical aggression was also directed at the children themselves:

> After my parents split up when I was four or five, my dad kept trying to break in. He threw us down the stairs and threw stuff at mum. He bashed her head against the wall (boy, 11).

> When my parents had a fight, dad hit mum and gave her a black eye. He left, but he's back now (boy, 10).

> My dad used to hit me and my mum, so we moved away. Then I went to stay with my dad and I wanted to stay with him. So my mum rejected me and vanished. I didn't know where she was. It was horrible. But it was brilliant with my dad. Now he's got a new girlfriend and it's all gone bad. He hits me, keeps me in, cuts off my money. I hate him. I want to go, but I've got nowhere to go. I don't want to go home at night (girl, 14).

Children and young people often attributed violent behaviour, particularly by fathers, to the influence of drink:

> It's always been the same, since I was about four. Dad comes in late and he's been drinking. He makes a lot of noise and mum asks him to quieten down. And then he either smashes the house up or hits my mum (girl, 15).

> After my dad left, my mum and me went to live with her brother. My uncle had about three women on the go but he used to expect mum to do everything round the house. When he came back drunk, he was always violent. He put my mum in hospital once with broken bones. He used to threaten me. We ran away with mum but he found us and smashed the place up ... (girl, 15).

In over a quarter of these 'worst experiences' concerning family violence, it was perpetrated by a stepfather against the child:

> If my step-dad had been drinking or had had a bad day at the betting shop he'd come home and lay into my mum and me. It used to get to me most when I walked to school with black eyes. I said I'd walked into a lamp-post. 'Cos dad had threatened me he'd kill me if I told anyone. I was terrified of him (girl, 16).

In six instances, children and young people alluded to direct and systematic physical and sexual abuse which had caused them unprecedented pain and terror. It is important to remember, however, that other young people had experienced similar abuse which was not considered by them to be their 'worst experience' — either they claimed to have 'got over it', or other prior or subsequent experiences had, in their eyes, been more traumatic.

Family break-up, new partners and bereavement

Family form and household structure in Britain today are considerably more varied than might be popularly imagined or politically welcome. Patterns of change may have been exaggerated and need to be balanced by patterns of continuity (Elliot 1986). For example, fewer people are now marrying (7.1 per 1000 eligible in 1981 to 6.8 per 1000 eligible in 1990), yet 85 per cent of families with dependent children are headed by a married couple; more children are being born outside of marriage, yet 78 per cent of all children are living with both of their birth parents (OPCS 1992). The death of the family has been much exaggerated and the reality is somewhat more complex. Even so, more and more children and young people are experiencing substantial disruptions in their family lives. Around one in three children under the age of 18 will experience divorce (Ayalon and Flasher 1993). As a result, significant proportions of children and young people are facing adaptation to new family forms. The experience of family break-ups and reformation is, therefore, within the indirect or direct experience of most children and young people.

Despite countervailing evidence pointing to the persisting trauma arising from the experience of divorce in children's lives (*ibid*), most of the children and young people in our study who had experienced high levels of family friction were often *relieved* when their birth parents split up. For others, such events were so far in the dim and distant past that they could not really remember them. Likewise, new partners of a birth parent (usually the mother) were often welcomed and contrasted favourably with the departed birth parent — 'mum's boyfriend is much better than my dad ever was' (girl, 11).

Nevertheless, 14 children and young people said that their parents splitting up had been their worst experience, particularly when they were required to make an active statement about where their loyalties lay:

> It was when my parents got divorced. I was so scared 'cos I thought I had to speak to the judge about who I wanted to live with — I didn't want to hurt anyone (girl, 12).

Many children and young people were clearly hostile to one birth parent or the other (usually the father) on account of their behaviour prior to separation or divorce and therefore found an expression of loyalty unproblematic. Yet when mothers acquired new partners, this obviously led to a renewed assessment of family relationships and dynamics, especially if there was real or perceived rejection of the child by the new partner, or a sudden decline in attention from the birth parent. However, only in three cases was the arrival of a new partner identified as the child's 'worst experience'. Many others, of course, were hardly enamoured by 'new partners' but had even worse experiences to talk about.

In four cases, the death of a parent or grandparent had been their most traumatic experience:

> It was when my dad died, after six years of leukemia. No-one had told me how bad he was. It was a big shock. I cried a lot (girl, 14).

Rape, sexual abuse and murder

Many children and young people have had a catalogue of negative experiences, any one of which might be identified by more 'ordinary kids' as highly troubling and traumatic. Yet, for a few, even these become overshadowed by some quite appalling experience. Within the 'sample' of young people interviewed, five disclosed the fact that they had been raped and one had been sexually abused by someone outside the family, and two had had their mothers murdered by their fathers. The girl who had been sexually abused observed:

> I still have nightmares. Something happened to me when I was six. It was a friend of the family who used to baby-sit for us. My mum says not to worry, 'he won't come back'. But I still worry. In my dreams, he still comes back (girl, 11).

One of the girls who had been raped by strangers described her experience as follows:

> Me and my friend got dragged on to a bus by these boys we sort of knew. We were screaming but people just watched — they probably thought it was a joke. At first we thought they were larking about, then we got terrified. They took us to an old caravan and threatened us with a bottle and raped us and made us do things we didn't want to do. I just wanted to be dead. I still feel like a dirty slag (girl, 15).

We must remind ourselves yet again that even this kind of awful personal degradation is not always viewed subjectively as the 'worst experience' of an individual's life, as the following comments made by a 15-year old girl suggests:

> I used to live with my nan. When I was just turned 14 I was raped by strangers. The police took me home and nan said she don't want me here any more. That's why I came into a home . . .
> But that wasn't really the worst thing. That could happen to anybody. It just happened to be me.
> The worst thing was when my dad hit me for no reason. I never understood it. He was my *dad*.

Other 'worst experiences'

The clusters of 'worst experiences' portrayed above are broken up by some 'one-off' and sometimes almost 'maverick' accounts which need to be included, if only to represent the diversity of experiences which can potentially deeply affect children's lives. A handful of young women talked about their suspected pregnancies and the fear, isolation and helplessness they experienced at the time:

> It was when I thought I was pregnant. I was only 14. I was scared to tell anyone. I didn't know what to do (girl, 15).

Two of the young people to whom we spoke had been traumatised through witnessing the physical deterioration of close relatives. One 10-year old boy had found the successive heart attacks of his grandmother hard to bear ('she used to walk around, now she's in a wheelchair'), while the other recounted:

It was meeting my mum when I was 12. She'd been in a mental hospital since I was born. I'd seen photos when she was young. She'd obviously got older but with medication and that — and her clothes — she looked so *old*. I was really shocked. And there was people laughing at her — I hated that.
And my dad had said she hated me but she said she loved me. I'm still wondering. It's made me very confused (girl, 15).

Another young person was continually troubled by:

always thinking what it'd be like with my real parents. My real mum was only 17 and probably knew she couldn't cope. I get on fine with my adoptive parents but I don't really talk much to them. I wonder if I would talk to my real mum (girl, 15).

The most bizarre but quite authentic 'worst experience' was recounted by a 10-year old girl whose grandmother had won an immense sum of money on the football pools:

She used to be really happy. Now all the neighbours have turned against her and she's always being pestered by reporters and begging letters. There's loads of bitchiness and she's not happy any more. It's made me really upset 'cos she's not like 'my nan' anymore.

Anticipated 'worst experiences' — anxieties and worries

As we have already illustrated, many of the children and young people interviewed, particularly those in the care system and from 'reconstituted' families, had already had all-too-real disturbing or traumatic experiences.

All children and young people were also asked what kinds of situations caused them anxiety or concern when they thought about the future. One might have expected general observations about topics such as the environment or conflict in the world. In fact, responses were firmly located within the personal contexts of their own lives.

Many of the young people expressed concerns about disease, death, unemployment, homelessness and violence, either affecting themselves or close members of their family. These worries were often represented in premonitions and nightmares, which were sometimes experienced with upsetting regularity. However, three broad areas of anxiety emerged. There was an overwhelming pre-occupation with accidents, death, separation and abandonment within the family:

> I get scared about my parents dying. I dream about it every night. It really scares me to think about that (boy, 13).

> I get really worried about my mum dying of cancer. She smokes a lot, although she's cut down because her boyfriend doesn't like it. If I joke about telling him, she doesn't like it. But although I make a joke of it, it really worries me (girl, 11).

> No real worries, man, except being abandoned by my family. Let's face it, people live for themselves. The reason I came into care was because I don't get on with my stepdad and I didn't see no-one for a year. He's more important to my mum than me. So she might decide she can do without me altogether. That *does* bother me (boy, 15).

The possibility of death or division in the family caused young people to contemplate what might happen to them — and few found comfort in positive scenarios about the support they might receive. For the majority, there was no substitute for the security which was provided by their parent or parents; even family contexts where friction, and even violence, was commonplace, were often preferable to any imagined alternative. Yet in such households, the likelihood of a split in the family in the future was obviously more likely, thus reinforcing and sharpening the anxieties of the children concerned:

> . . . all the arguing between my parents and between them and me. Sometimes I think it's my fault. I get worried about them splitting up. And then I get angry and upset: if they did, what will happen to me? (boy, 10).

The second major area of anxiety was bullying at school. Many of the children, as we have reported, already had direct experience of bullying. Many others worried about it happening to them in the future, particularly those soon moving on to secondary school: 'being bullied and teased at comp, 'cos you're only a small fish in a big pond' (boy, 10). The folklore, as much as the realities, of the victimisation of newcomers to secondary school was a constant source of anxiety amongst children in their final year of junior school:

> I get all sweaty when I think about going to comp. I get worried

about getting picked on and coping socially. It'll probably be
OK, but you still get worried (girl, 10).

Clearly it is impossible to know which individuals will emerge as
the bullies and which as the bullied in secondary school, but the
prevalence of bullying in schools is now well documented (see Skinner 1992, Tattum 1993) and it remains a source of preoccupation
well into secondary school life even if bullying has not yet taken
place:

> All the time I see other kids getting bullied at school. They get
> pushed around and money taken from them. Some kids get
> picked on a lot but you never really know if it'll be your turn
> next. I get really worried that I'm going to be the next one to be
> beaten up (boy, 13).

The third major area of worry was a sense of 'sexual vulnerability' amongst young women, anxieties which seemed to start
around the age of 10/11 and which became more profound as girls
entered their teens. Being raped or assaulted was a general fear
which found specific expression in the physical environment of the
local neighbourhood: dimly lit streets, the wasteland by the youth
club, the open space in the park, the woods near home. As young
women become aware of their own sexuality and start to experience
being treated as sexual 'objects' through the passing comments of
young and older men, they also become 'tuned in' to such locations
as being the sorts of places where women tend to be assaulted. Once
the fears are established, they can become all pervasive:

> I keep thinking that one day I'm going to get raped. It preys on
> your mind. When I'm out, I'm always thinking someone is
> following me. When I'm by the woods I think someone is going
> to jump out on me. Even when I'm in the house on my own, I
> think there's someone in the next room. It's really frightening
> (girl, 13).

> You see gangs of boys who call you names and sometimes you
> wonder what they're going to do next. And men by the pub
> looking at you. I get frightened. I know it sounds stupid but
> when I walk past trees I can see hands reaching out at me,
> trying to drag me in. Maybe I've watched too many horror
> films! (girl, 14).

The depth of such fears needs to be placed in the context of
broader social attitudes and responses to young women who persist
in walking past trees, through woods or across wasteland — if something does happen to them, the finger is pointed at them — by
family, friends and strangers alike — for 'contributory negligence'

(see Herbert 1989). The process of 'blaming the victim' is common-place; the general message conveyed through the media, local com-munities and family contexts is, too often, that women behaving in this way were 'asking for it'. Such attitudes, which were commonly held to be the stance adults would take (see Chapter 4), are hardly conducive to young women expressing such anxieties. Many feel all they can do is keep them to themselves and 'cry in the night'. We discuss issues around adults 'listening' or, too often not listening, or being perceived by children and young people as incapable of listen-ing or understanding in Chapter 4.

The anxieties about the future experienced by children and young people are naturally bound up with their specific personal circumstances. One girl had a younger sister facing an imminent heart operation; her worries, not surprisingly, were currently exclus-ively focused on the operation going wrong. Similarly, one boy had an older brother in the army who had just started a tour of Northern Ireland and he was deeply concerned about him getting shot. Other young people (such as a girl with alopecia) had recurrent anxieties about the responses of others to certain physical characteristics. Another girl, for example, said:

I worry about getting rid of my warts before going to comp.
The other kids have got used to it here. It's OK. But at comp, they'll pick on me. I'll get teased (girl, 11).

We might note that this book can only communicate through the medium of the written word. Here the word 'teased' may sound somewhat trivial but it was not when coupled with the worried expression on the face of the girl concerned. This raises significant questions about the use of children's language: at least in certain situations, it can convey very different meanings to those attached to the same words by adults.

Surprisingly, very few children and young people referred to issues around their peer group as a source of anxiety. A few mid-teenage young people expressed concern about not fitting in with the crowd and even fewer claimed to be anxious about being separated from or losing contact with their friends. Some said that what troubled them most about the future was whether or not they would manage to get a girlfriend or boyfriend. Such preoccupations clearly become more prevalent amongst older teenagers, as the peer group assumes a relatively greater importance in their lives and young people seek to secure a greater measure of independence from their families.

Only one refreshingly optimistic individual claimed to worry about *nothing*: 'just let life go on — there's nothing to worry about if you're good' (girl, 10).

Commentary

There are a number of observations to be made from this depiction of the 'worst' things experienced by children and young people. Clearly they take diverse forms and are located on a very broad continuum of severity to the dispassionate eye; nonetheless, they are *all* very real and troubling to the children who have experienced them, as their accounts indicate.

It is noticeable that racism is conspicuous by its absence. Although 74 children and young people were from minority ethnic backgrounds or of mixed race, only two specifically identified racism as their worst experience. One might suspect, however, that at least some of the bullying and name-calling described by a substantial minority of all children and young people had racist overtones, even if this was not detected or perceived by the children concerned, or revealed to a white, male researcher (Troyna and Hatcher 1992).

It is particularly important to note that it was not always the originating problem which in fact caused the 'worst experience' but the sequence of difficulties *associated* with it. One 11-year old boy was deeply concerned about arguments between his parents because he was worried it would cut off contact with his grandparents, to whom he was very close. Similarly, a nine-year old girl said that violence between her mother and her aunt made her worry that 'I might never see my cousins again'.

An 11-year old boy in care identified his constant changes of school as his worst experience, not because of the educational difficulties this caused but because each time he had to go through the process of explaining why he was in care and then having to deal with the consequences of that. A 15-year old girl described the violence between her parents, but it was really the sense of helplessness and lack of understanding which caused it to be such an awful experience:

> My mum and dad were always fighting but I didn't know why. I was sometimes in the room but it was like I wasn't there. I was completely shut out. I didn't know what was going on. I used to get really worried. I was gutted. It was really horrible. My sister never did nothing so it was down to me. But I didn't know what to do . . .

By far the most graphic and emotive account of the *sequential* nature of a 'worst experience' was provided by a 12-year old boy in care:

> The worst thing was my mum dying. She always had a lot of headaches 'cos my dad used to hit her about when he was

drunk. One day she got a blood clot behind her eye and had a
brain haemorrhage. I can't remember much how I felt, but I do
think about it sometimes . . .

My sisters went to live with my auntie, 'cos she had a spare
room for them. But there wasn't any room for me. I came here
because I had no-where else to go. That's really the worst
thing . . .

For this young man, it is the feeling of disbelief, rejection and
isolation rather than his mother's death *per se* which constitutes his
worst experience.

We have seen from this chapter that children and young people
inhabit some very different social worlds, some characterised by
apparent support and security and some riddled with endemic
violence and victimisation. Virtually all, however, have experienced
situations which have left them troubled and disturbed, some
obviously far more so than others. But quite how each of these
experiences has affected the individual concerned is virtually impossible to fathom simply through a dispassionate professional
analysis. Accounts of name-calling in school were sometimes more
emotive and upsetting than accounts of violence and abuse by young
people with greater 'natural' or socialised resilience.

Only by listening to the *meaning* imputed to such experiences by
the young people concerned can those seeking to support them
secure a measure of understanding of how they are affecting them.
An expanded awareness of what actually troubles children and
young people may lead to a more sensitive and appropriate response
to particular individuals. Name calling, for example, does hurt. It
might not hurt an adult to the same degree (possibly) and the hurt is
not as serious as the potential hurt caused by other forms of abuse
towards children. However, to deny the pain it *can* cause in the face
of what children and young people actually say is to demean children, disregard the validity of *their* accounts, and thereby perpetuate
the communication gap that not only exists, but appears to be growing, between children and adults.

Similarly, and more seriously, on what basis do we allocate
resources to the protection of children from abuse and deny
resources to combat playground bullying? We do not suggest that
bullying and child abuse, as conventionally defined, are equivalent,
although extreme forms of bullying have led to the death of children,
but we would contend that *both* contribute substantially to the
unhappy lives of many children and both require a response by
adults.

Furthermore, most children have a range of private anxieties
about the future, some of which concern them a great deal.

Whether in terms of current or potential difficulties, the *opportunity* for children and young people to share such experiences — on their terms — is critical for them to be able to cope with them. The capacity to deal with them is often contingent upon adult support, yet, as we argue in Chapter 4, many children and young people are cautious, reluctant and even fearful about discussing such issues with anyone, let alone adults who might potentially be able to help. This, we contend, is because they anticipate eliciting reactions which, to them, are inappropriate, misguided and, critically, beyond their control.

4 Adults listening

'Freedom, to the adolescent, looks suspiciously like neglect'. So argued Pitt-Aikens and Thomas Ellis (1990) in their book about the causes of delinquency, but the assertion could be extended to other aspects of young people's lives. It is a contentious point but, from an ever younger age, children and young people are apparently seeking a public sense of independence. More privately, the worlds of adolescents remain complex and confusing and few young people would maintain that it is easy to resolve many of the problematics they encounter without the help, support or advice of others. Some, of course, have little choice but to try to sort things out for themselves. Most would prefer to consult and discuss issues with others — but which others? On what basis?

We have a vast literature on adolescence which draws attention to the processes by which young people move from dependent childhood to independent adulthood — from the cocoon of family life, through the framework of the teenage peer group, to allegedly self-sufficient 'maturity'. We also have growing trends which speak of experiential learning and empowering young people, yet much of this is relatively empty rhetoric which lacks theoretical or empirical substance. The sweeping generalisations which are often attached to such rhetorical assertions fail to concede any 'horses for courses' arguments: namely that children and young people, like all people, sometimes seek to act with high levels of autonomy and sometimes wish to place decision-making in the hands of others (for a sophisticated, detailed, analysis of this point, see Rutter and Rutter 1992). Of course, many children do talk frequently to their parents, but conversely there are things they would not wish to confide in them. Teenagers may display an explicit faith in the integrity of their 'mates', but conversely the facts of peer group pressure may cause them to be reticent about other matters (particularly matters around sexuality and gender relationships which depart from dominant cultural norms, see Mac an Ghaill 1994). Children and young people may see a value in confiding in the range of professional adults with whom they are in routine contact (such as teachers, and perhaps social workers or youth workers), but conversely they may not do so because they may hold too many suspicions about how they will react. Rees, in his study of young people who run away from home, suggests that 'some young people seemed to have given up hope in a positive response from adults', using the following quotation to illustrate his point:

> I was just feeling depressed, really lonely, so like I was crying out for help and everyone just turned their back on me, you know, my teachers, my social workers, nobody wanted to know ... I was at rock bottom ... 'cause I'd totally lost my confidence in adults completely (Rees 1993, p.74).

His conclusion to what was in many respects a very different study, relates closely to our own findings:

> Young people who have lost their faith in adults in this way must be even more vulnerable to mistreatment and abuse as they are unlikely to feel there is any point in turning to anyone for help (*ibid*, p.74).

Numerous theories exist which seek to explain the processes of development during adolescence and youth, and the factors which may influence such processes both constructively and negatively. Some such theories focus exclusively on the individual while others locate individual development within the social, and sometimes socio-political, context. Havighurst (1972) has attempted to reconcile the 'personal and social learning tasks of adolescence', while work by Coffield *et al.* (1986) has built on the class cultural analyses developed by youth cultural analysts during the 1970s (see Brake 1980) in order to establish a more empirically-based account of social and cultural reproduction.

Although the intellectual traditions from which such theories derive may be very different, particularly in the emphases given to internal forces over external ones, or vice versa, the message conveyed is often very similar. There may be doubt cast on the rigid 'Sturm und Drang' (storm and stress) hypothesis propounded in the early psychology of adolescence (Stanley Hall 1904), but few would dispute that late childhood and adolescence is a turbulent stage in the life-cycle, even if most young people continue to subscribe to ordinary, conventional and conservative values (Davis 1990) rather than to the cultural resistance and rebellion ascribed to them by more radical sociologists and social theorists (see Hall and Jefferson 1978).

What is also clear is that a variety of social pressures and changes in child-rearing practices have foreshortened the period of life when a young person is truly a child (Hendry *et al.* 1993), even if social policy changes have also extended the duration of adolescence and deferred the passage to adulthood, so that a growing minority of young adults become 'trapped as teenagers' (Williamson 1985, 1993). Hendry *et al.* maintain that today's child 'in some senses at least has entered upon adolescence long before leaving primary school' (1993, p.1).

Most evidence points towards the remarkable resilience of children and young people in adjusting to the various pressures that they face: in relation to the formation of gender roles and relationships with the opposite sex; in dealing with acceptance and rejection within the peer group; and with regard to gradually securing independence from their parents. The capacity to cope effectively with such pressures does, however, depend upon the extent to which they are concentrated all at one time. Young people who, for whatever reason, have more than one issue to cope with at any one time are most likely to have problems of adjustment. Such problems will be exacerbated when there is conflict between roles ascribed to the individual by self and by significant others. This issue is particularly pertinent to our argument since, despite Coleman and Hendry's (1990) contention that young people can pace themselves through adolescent transitions and be active agents in their own development, there is clearly a need for them to draw on the support, advice and guidance of others. Where the relationship between individual children and those others is subject to 'dissonance', the desired outcomes are unlikely to materialise, resulting in a loss of faith or trust in those others and a strong likelihood of children falling back on their own resources, whether they are adequate or not. The long-term consequences of failing to deal effectively with personal troubles are that young people are in fact *less* in control of their lives (however much they may claim that they are), causing further complications in their personal and social relationships and damage to their self-esteem. The more resourceful will adopt a range of strategies for dealing with threatening or troubling situations (see Covington and Beery 1977). We should not romanticise this in terms which suggest that they have managed to 'cope', however. Coping — through the use of a repertoire of psychological defences (Kaplan 1980) — is a very different matter from exercising personal autonomy on the basis of access to a range of personal and material resources capable of 'empowering' children and young people to make balanced choices and judgements about their futures.

Who do children talk to?

This chapter discusses *who* young people talk to about their negative experiences and anxieties, *why* they have 'selected' those individuals and *what* they expect from sharing their concerns with them.

This is a complex area to explore. The initial research question related both to who *do* young people talk to when they have bad experiences or worries and to whom would young people talk to should such circumstances arise. The question therefore opened the door for both factual and speculative responses. And, of course, 'it all depends'. It depends on the issue, it depends on who you feel you can trust and it depends on what you want from the sharing of a confidence — to unload a burden, to be assisted in finding a solution or to have them resolve the problem.

Friends might fulfil the first function and possibly the second. Parents, relatives and professionals would be more likely to fulfil the second and third — or so young people might hope. All this is, to a large extent, predictable. It was therefore all the more surprising that over a quarter of children and young people held a strong conviction that they would talk to no-one. Many other young people said that they would only very reluctantly discuss their personal circumstances with others.

No-one

You learn to get by (boy, 15).

Never talk to anyone about personal things. Never liked talking, never will. Talked to you because everybody is and they said you was OK. Have always looked after myself and will continue to do so (girl, 15).

Because of the deep-rooted scepticism amongst children and young people about the capacity of others to provide relevant or acceptable advice and support, it is important to discuss this theme in some detail.

Many young people simply had *no trust* in other people, whether friends of the same age, or adults:

I don't talk to people but I do get bothered about things — then I blow up and get into trouble. But I want to sort things out myself. Don't trust no-one else. I've survived once, so I'll survive again. I've grown up the hard way. I know how to get by (boy, 15).

I don't tell nobody 'cos I can't trust anyone in my life any more.
No-one believes me. There's no point (boy, 10).

Keep it to yourself, that's the best way. Don't trust other
people, they blab, man. They tell other people. And then they
laugh at you (boy, 11).

If you tell anyone about it, it might get out of hand. They'll
twist your story. It's better to sort it out your own way (girl,
14).

Others felt it was fairly pointless talking to others, even if they
trusted them. There was little purpose in doing so because they had
little confidence that anyone else could help them sort things out:

You'd feel embarrassed. They'd think you're stupid. They
wouldn't really understand. They probably couldn't do much
anyway. I prefer to sort myself out (girl, 13).

The 'they' in these references remains mysterious, but it is essentially a reference to all other personal contacts: peer group friends,
family, and professional 'others'. The bottom line for these young
people is that, ultimately, you do have to sort *yourself* out, so why
even bother telling anyone else in the first place, especially when
'their' reaction is unpredictable and may potentially not even be
constructive (in the eyes of the individual concerned):

It's no use telling anybody else. I just hope things will go away,
but sometimes they get worse. But they might get worse even if
I told someone else. No-one can do anything about it — except
me (boy, 12).

This abject lack of confidence in the capacity of others to, first,
be trusted and, secondly, offer appropriate ideas or courses of action
was repeated so often that further verbatim comments are worth
including to reinforce the point:

I get by on my own — I'll have to in the future. I've had to
learn to look after myself. I'm used to it (boy, 15).

Don't talk to anyone — just go off in a mood or watch TV.
They wouldn't listen. Don't need anyone (boy, 11).

No, 'cos they'd probably get me wrong. I don't want to be
helped. I just want to be left alone and sort things out myself
(boy, 11).

I just talk to myself, to get it out of my system. There's no
point in talking to anyone else . . . 'cos they'd probably tease
you and think you were silly (girl, 10).

Nobody. I just sit on my bed and talk to myself. Grown-ups
don't take you seriously. They just say 'Good, good, good', 'cos
they're not really that bothered. And I don't really trust my
friends; they'd never keep a secret . . . (boy, 10).

Just keep it in and bottle it up. I wouldn't really know who to
tell, because I don't know who I could trust. I suppose it would
depend on what the problem was. Maybe I'd talk to my friends,
or maybe my parents — but you don't know how they'd react.
If it was, like, about bullying, my dad'd probably go steaming
in head first and make things worse, so I probably wouldn't
bother . . . (boy, 13).

No-one. You have to try and sort things out yourself before it
gets worse. There's no other way (girl, 14).

Two brief observations are noteworthy here. First, many more
boys than girls said that they talked to no-one. It might be alleged
that their apparent 'independence' was a typical macho 'bravado',
which might possibly crumble in the face of real adversity. But, even
when probed, they were adamant that they invariably kept things to
themselves. Yet despite this assertion that the only way was to sort
things out themselves, many were not confident that they were likely
to do this constructively. Younger male children in particular said
that their response was, more often than not, to 'run and hide' —
retreating to bedrooms and in front of Nintendo screens. Older ones
projected a more confrontational stance, emphasising the need to
'fight back' in whatever way was possible or necessary and never,
never risk being perceived as weak or lacking control. Such 'hard
shells' concealed the anxieties that nevertheless existed. It was conceded that these were addressed, often inadequately, in the private
spheres of their lives, but there was no way that they would be
admitted in public, either to friends, family or professionals:

— No, I don't talk to no-one about it.
Interviewer: So how do you deal with it, or don't those things
bother you any more?
— Yeah, man, they still bother me. But I just keep it all
banged up inside me and then I let it all out and bash
something — or myself. But not when anyone's around. I try to
keep out of people's way if I'm going to crack, 'cos I might bash
them. But I never go to my bedroom because I'd smash it up,
and I don't want to do that (boy, 15).

— I don't tell anybody because I can't trust anyone in my life
any more. No-one believes me. I don't know why . . .

Interviewer: But you've told me you've had all sorts of problems over the years.
— Yeah, and I've been suicidal loads of times. But you have to sort things out for yourself. I ain't saying I don't get bothered about things. What I'm saying is that I can't see there's anyone I could turn to who'd really take me seriously and be able to help me sort things out (boy, 10).

— I turn to myself and try and sort things through. There's people around who say they want to help me, but I'd prefer not to have them poking their nose in. I don't need no-one.
Interviewer: Don't you think that those sort of people might be able to help you, at least think things through — like, someone to bounce your thoughts off?
— Yeah, well I've got enough thoughts in my head that need bouncing! But they just ain't that bothered. They don't listen. They don't understand. What do they really know about *me*? (boy, 13).

Cats, dogs and 'cockerels'

It sounds a bit silly, but I talk to my dog (girl, 10).

Half a dozen children and young people argued, with a modicum of embarrassment but a fair degree of persuasion, that they confided only in their pets. This permitted them to talk things through, get things off their chest and consider how to deal with anxieties, without fear of 'betrayal' or inappropriate reactions. The only problem with the dog, one 10-year old girl observed, was that 'he keeps walking off'. Other children's similar strategies were to talk to imaginary friends and inanimate objects including, in the case of one fanatical Tottenham Hotspur supporter, 'my Spurs cockerel' (10-year old boy).

Friends

Over a quarter of the children and young people interviewed said that they would usually share experiences and anxieties with close friends whom they trusted. Rarely did they expect friends to come up with any answers although, for older young people, best friends sometimes did provide new ideas:

Some of my friends see a way out. They help me to see new angles on things (girl, 15).

More often, close friends were confided in because they would understand and could be trusted 'not to spread it around'. Talking to friends was a means of unloading troubles, getting things off your chest and, perhaps, hearing another point of view. But there were no great expectations that friends could actively assist in resolving problems or even, generally, suggest ways of doing so. You still had to sort things out yourself. The main purpose of talking to trustworthy friends was to use them to 'soak up' your worries:

> Mainly friends I trust. 'Cos they can soak up my worries and that makes me feel better. But they can't really do nothing about them (girl, 13).

Family

Excluding those children in the care system who were cut off from their families (and the majority were not completely cut off) and the significant minority of all children and young people who were adamant that they would talk to no-one, the majority of children and young people identified one individual *within the family network* — most frequently 'mum' — as the person with whom they would share confidences and talk through their anxieties. (This confirms a view expressed in the DES 1982 report, *Young People in the 1980s.*) Brothers, sisters, brothers' girlfriends, sisters' boyfriends and, less often, uncles, aunts and parents' friends and neighbours also played their part.

The reasons for selecting particular individuals as special confidant were varied, starting with basic requirements of listening and understanding, but also deriving from more sophisticated criteria such as shared experiences and the quality of advice such individuals were perceived to provide:

> I talk to my mum. I know it sounds a bit soppy, but she went through it as well. My dad was a bastard to both of us (boy, 15)

> My mum appreciates being informed. I think she'd be really upset if I didn't talk to her. So she listens carefully to the things I tell her and she never has a go at me. And she comes up with good ideas about what to do. I think she understands me well. It's like we're on the same wavelength when I talk to her (girl, 14).

Children and young people and their confidants were not always on the same wavelength. One 14-year old boy had discussed being bullied at school with his older brother, hoping for some constructive advice — 'all he said was "don't be a weed, knock 'em out and put 'em in hospital". That wasn't much help'.

Here lies the problem. Despite this network of apparent support upon which young people could draw, very few said they would feel comfortable with or automatically approach adults in the event of experiencing difficulties. They generally felt uncomfortable about the reaction they would receive and therefore were inclined to communicate anxieties only as a last resort, when they were in a position of some desperation. The doubts and reservations held by children and young people about adult responses are discussed more fully later in this chapter. They applied even more so to adult professionals with whom these young people were in regular contact, raising *a priori* questions about the capacity of professional strangers to command or inspire any trust or confidence in many children and young people, which is clearly the basis of any free and willing disclosure of information.

Expert listeners?

Of the 46 young people accommodated in the care system, who did not have the same frequency of contact with family networks as other children, eight said that they would discuss their problems with *specific* individuals on the residential care staff. Only two felt confident in, and comfortable with their field social workers. This confirms the recent findings of the Dolphin Project, in which one young person was noted as saying,

> Social workers . . . they sit in the office . . . moving all the kids around . . . people who actually work in children's home and do all the dirty work. I think they understand' (The Dolphin Project 1994, p.35).

Eight other children and young people from the wider sample trusted particular teachers at their schools and four others said that they would turn to other professionals, such as a youth worker.

However, along with many other young people who had more forthright suspicions about talking to adults and particularly professionals, even these young people expressed general reservations and did not feel relaxed about seeking such support. They felt that neither teachers nor social workers could keep their mouths shut and that there was always a danger of them 'blabbing'. So even discussion with those they apparently trusted was approached with caution:

> The care staff talk to us and some of them are safe. But we don't volunteer *nothing* (boy, 14).

The frequent use of the concept of 'safe', as used in the vernacular by some young people, is interesting: it refers to being 'cool' and 'OK' but it also conveys a sense of trust and, literally, safety. It is often used in drug-dealing and delinquent circles as a testimonial to individuals who can be trusted not to 'split' or 'grass'.

Some of them are all right. But you never know, they might
grass or they might not grass — so it's better not to say
anything. If they press you to talk, I just make up some mad
story (boy, 14).

This jaded cynicism of professionals was occasionally compensated
by testimony to the potential of similar professional support:

The care staff here are brilliant. There's always someone to talk
to. And, if not, I'd talk to my teachers. School is bang on —
it's great. You've heard what I've been through, but I've never
missed a day (girl, 15).

How do adults react?

Most professionals and many non-professional adults will claim that
they attempt to approach supporting children and young people in
ways which are consistent with the attributes and processes desired
by young people. Why, then, do children feel so differently about
adult support and intervention?

A substantial number of young people, as noted already, simply
believe that enlisting adult support of any kind is pointless because,
ultimately, one has to face up to problems alone:

No use, no point. You have to find ways of dealing with things
yourself. No-one else can do it for you (boy, 13).

Others had a spectrum of different reasons for suspecting the value
of adult support.

One might surmise that clear distinctions would be made between observations about *professional* support and assessments of
more general, often *parental*, support. The themes raised by young
people were, however, consistent across both groups of adults except
where the structural nature of contact was clearly different — in
other words, professionals had more infrequent contact with children and young people premised upon a specific *professional* task
(teaching, social work, youth work). This, in itself, invoked scepticism on the part of many children and young people:

Too often another kid is just another case (boy, 17).

They come in and out of your life, but they can go home at the
end of the day — you've got to deal with things *all* of the time
(boy, 14).

They're not really that bothered — it's just a job to them (girl,
13).

Furthermore, young people with direct experience of professional 'support' alleged that there wasn't much point in trying to cultivate trust and confidence in them because 'they're always moving on' (girl, 15).

Specific criticisms were levelled at parents for different reasons, usually relating to the fact that they were too busy to listen:

> Parents ignore you. They don't show any interest in you and then they blame you when things go wrong (girl, 12).

> Parents don't listen — it's always 'tell me later, I'm busy right now'. They're not bothered (boy, 10).

Other reservations applied to both parents and professionals, though not always in equal measure; where the weight of criticism was attached predominantly to one group or the other, this will be noted in the text.

Lack of understanding/incapable of understanding

Children and young people are acutely aware that they inhabit a very different world from that in which the previous generation grew up. This led a number of children and young people to assert that adults — *all adults* — were incapable of really *understanding* their experiences and concerns, all the more so if there was only occasional contact with them:

> *Re: social workers*
> They do one good thing for you and two things bad. You don't know where you stand. They go on about knowing what's best for you, but it's all out of books. How can they know your 'best interests' when they don't even know you?
> What kind of contact do social workers have with their kids? One visit in two or three months? Nothing at all.
> I know they're trying to do their best for you. But they haven't been through what you've been through. So they'll never know, they'll *never* understand (girl, 14).

> They talk to you and try to get round your problems but they don't understand. They don't know nothing about what it's really like for you (boy, 15).

> *Re: parents*
> They don't listen. You can't get through to them. Times have changed since they were young but they see things like it was then.
>   They don't understand what things are like now . . . No-one's on our side (girl, 15).

Impose their own views

This perceived lack of understanding is often reinforced by an additional perception that adults make little effort to listen. This, in turn, leads them to construct their own views on a situation which derives from 'their opinion, not ours' (boy, 13). What is then commonly reflected — explicitly or implicitly — back to young people is not an apparently accurate grasp of *their* experience or feelings, but a 'distorted' version which has been corrupted by adult misinterpretation. The concept of 'contributory negligence' on the part of young women facing sexual harassment is but an extreme example of this process:

> *Re: social workers*
> They don't really listen. And then they don't believe you. My mum is mentally disturbed. And because I wouldn't talk to them — I mean, I've always kept people at a distance, that's just the way *I* am — they thought I was disturbed, like mum. When I told them about being raped, they put it down to my imagination. Why should I imagine *that*? But he's owned up now. But no-one believed me. Social workers don't listen. They see what they want to see. They don't want to *know* (girl, 17).

> If you tell people the whole truth, it might get out of hand. They twist the story. And then they try to sort it out *their* way (girl, 14).

> *Re: parents*
> Some listen to you. The trouble is they only see things from their own point of view (girl, 15).

> I had this fight at school and got sent home. It was the first time I'd ever had a fight and I was really upset. Dad wasn't bothered at first — he said talk to mum. Then he came in and said 'Did you win?' . . .
> Adults don't understand kids' reasons, they don't hear their explanations — kids don't *win*. It's bad for both of you, but somehow you both end up fighting at the time. He's my mate. But I couldn't get a word in edgeways. My dad only wanted to know bits of the story — the bits he'd understand. He's stubborn. He didn't want to listen. And when he'd heard what *he* wanted to hear, he changed the subject. He didn't want to listen to what *I* wanted to say (boy, 13).

Breach confidentiality

A central platform of children's doubts about adult support (and indeed, about sharing confidences with friends) was that they 'spread things around': 'the whole world knows' (girl, 10). This is a terrible indictment of any adults who commit themselves to confidentiality but is a particularly caustic allegation for professionals for whom confidentiality is central to their ethics. Nonetheless, there is a pervasive feeling amongst children and young people that even a commitment to confidentiality is, too often, a 'false promise' and that information divulged will then be 'spread around' without the consent of the individual concerned.

Some young people had developed strategies to test the water. One 14-year old girl, when asked who she would seek support from if existing networks proved inadequate, said:

> I suppose I might ask for advice from social workers or a teacher, but you don't know who they'd tell. I'd probably test them out with small things and see how fast other people found out.

A 10-year old girl, presented with a similar question, commented:

> I'd be too scared to. You don't know them. You don't know whether they're going to cheat on you.

The use of the word 'scared' in this context is clearly cause for concern. It was repeated on a number of occasions by children and young people:

> I'm scared of telling adults — in case it goes further. The teachers would probably talk about it in the staff room (girl, 15).

We have noted already the reticence of many children and young people to talk to any adults because 'they blab, man'. The prevailing belief amongst children and young people is that professionals have an unerring capacity to 'gossip'. This view derives perhaps from the accurate perception that much of their work is largely about *talk* and children fail to distinguish between idle chatter and professional communication, as the following comment suggests with a concluding ironic twist:

> Sometimes social workers tell you personal things about themselves. I think they're trying to get you to trust them. But are they true? How do you know? And then they say things like 'Can you keep a secret?' and you think this is because they want you to tell them your secrets. If they're telling me secrets, they'll probably tell mine to somebody else. They're loudmouths (girl, 11).

Finally, a paradox within all this emphasis by young people on confidentiality and their suspicion of frequent breaches by professionals was revealed in a group interview with teenage girls:

— I'd talk to Miss ——— (teacher). She's got her head
  screwed on. She's caring and she'd be confidential about it.
— And she's got her own problems which she told in
  confidence to some of the students in the sixth form.
— Yeah, and *they* told the whole school!

Inappropriate reactions

The most encompassing basis for doubting the value of adult intervention was the experience and anticipation of it being inappropriate — not what was expected or desired (and young people said that adult reactions were invariably inappropriate — one way or the other). Both involved not being taken seriously, not being listened to or understood and not being consulted on what course of action, if any, should be taken. One, however, was about trivialising issues; the other was about over-reaction which was perceived by children as often counter-productive and not usually, from their point of view, in their best interests:

Trivialise

People treat you as a joke. They don't take you seriously (boy, 13).

Parents don't take things seriously. They just tell you to grow up (girl, 14).

When I'm at the bus stop some of the other kids call me 'snob' and it gets to me. Mum just says 'Ignore them' and dad says 'Stop being a weed and get on with it'. They don't take it seriously (boy, 11).

Mums are a bit more understanding. Dads just treat things as a laugh. They won't admit to their experiences, but I bet they had the same worries when they were kids. So they just joke about things that we want them to treat seriously (boy, 12).

I wouldn't talk to the staff here. They don't treat me seriously. And I don't trust social workers. Just because I put on a friendly smiley face they don't realise I want them to be serious with me (boy, 12).

Sometimes they take you seriously but a lot of the time they just laugh at you (boy, 9).

For others, the pendulum was perceived to swing suddenly from an attitude that trivialised experiences and concerns (epitomised by the expression 'why don't you grow up?') to one which over-reacted and adopted an over-protective and disempowering stance:

> Adults keep on joking about it but sometimes they suddenly realise it is serious and then they go over the top (girl, 10).

Over-reaction

It is one thing treating a child's problems and concerns seriously; it is quite another to then decide how to 'deal' with it, irrespective of the child's wishes. Adults were seen to have a tendency to 'dive in head first' and pursue a course of action which young people did not always seek and which they remained unconvinced would yield productive outcomes:

> If you tell your teacher or your parents you are getting picked on by other kids, they go in head first and that makes things worse. When I told my dad I was being bullied, he came steaming down to the school and the teacher had a go at these kids. But they just picked on me worse 'cos they thought it was a laugh that I'd had to tell my dad (boy, 13).

A more appropriate response to a similar situation was described by a 13-year old girl:

> I was getting called names at school and I talked to my mum about it. She said she understood 'cos it had happened to her. I didn't know that, but it made me feel better. She asked me if I wanted her to do anything and she offered to come to the school, but I said No. Sometimes that can make matters worse.

Such accounts were exceptional as young people struggled to depict appropriate responses to their troubles. More often, they ended up recounting more tales of inappropriate reactions:

> When my mum and dad was fighting I talked to my nan about it. I didn't want her to do anything. I just wanted to tell someone and I'd always got on with my nan. But she went and had a go at my mum for upsetting me and then my mum had a go at me for telling nan which she says I shouldn't have done. So it made everything worse. I think nan got the wrong impression. She didn't really understand (girl, 9).

I suppose they care about you. But they make a fuss and go
over the top. Sometimes you only want to talk (girl, 10).

Here we have situations in which adults decide that something
must be done. Clearly, there are circumstances when this has to be,
and this may be against the wishes of the child, although it is imperative that there is absolute clarity about why this has to be and that
such situations are kept to a minimum. When at all possible, it does
seem to be important to establish with children why they are sharing
their concerns and to negotiate a desirable and effective course of
action.

The worst form of over-reaction by adults is when it is perceived
to rebound on children themselves and a process is invoked which,
in essence, is about 'blaming the victim':

Me and my friends always used to hang around in the park.
One day there was this man there. He wasn't doing anything
but he spooked me. He was there every day for about a week.
So I told my mum. I got grounded for a month! It was like it
was my fault. I wish I hadn't told her now (girl, 14).

This regret about having talked to adults on account of their
failure to listen, understand and react 'appropriately' was echoed
repeatedly. Young people would be more careful next time. In
effect, this closes off avenues of communication between children
and those who may be in a good position to help and support them.
But children didn't want 'lectures'; they wanted discussion and consultation. They did not want adults to jump to conclusions; they
wanted to check and have confirmed that their accounts had been
properly heard and interpreted. Then a mutually acceptable course
of action could be agreed.

Children were, by and large, quite willing to acknowledge that
adults were *well-intentioned* ('I know they are doing it for our own
good, but it doesn't seem like that' — girl, 11). They also accepted
that adults faced dilemmas in deciding how to respond ('if they
didn't do anything, we'd think they didn't care' — girl, 15). But it
was the unpredictability, contradictory and sometimes hypocritical
nature of their responses which engendered enormous confusion in
children. One minute they were being told to 'Grow up', the next
that they weren't old enough to exercise autonomy. One minute they
were being told that they'd have to sort things out themselves, the
next somebody else was sorting it out for them — without any
consultation.

It was these issues which made many children and young people
wary of talking to adults. If you could not be sure how they would
respond, it was better not to say anything at all.

So why talk?

It should disturb all of us, whether we work with children professionally or not, that so many children and young people seem
reluctant to talk to anyone about their difficulties. We may understand some of the reasons for this if we consider why children and
young people should want to communicate their anxieties at all.
Securing some grasp of the rationale for talking starts to clarify why
young people talk to some individuals and not others.

There are three basic reasons why young people (no differently
from *all* people) elect to share their experiences and worries:

- to 'unload';
- to elicit ideas and possible choices for action;
- to catalyse action by others.

As has been noted already, young people are only too starkly
aware that, ultimately, it is *their own* actions which are most likely to
bring about the change needed to address negative experiences or
eliminate anxieties. Thus the first two reasons are by far the most
important. Young people do not seek or expect action by others
unless they ask for it. Broadly, they seek to *unload* problems on friends
and seek *advice*, *information* and *guidance* from adults. (Younger
children are more likely to believe and hope that others can 'sort
things out' on their behalf, but even the 8/9-year olds we interviewed
still felt that they had to take most of the initiative on those matters
which concerned them most.)

The dilemma for children and young people, as they see it, is that
once they convey something to adults, the power to determine what
should then be done is — too often — taken out of their hands.

The issue of confidentiality is central here. We have already
made some observations, in relation to the position of the social
researcher (see Chapter 2), about the difficulties that face adults in
making decisions about how to respond when they are put in possession of guilty, dangerous or 'risky' knowledge. How far can such
knowledge remain confidential in a social work context?

Without experience of credible and reliable assurances of confidentiality, many children and young people, it seems, will not trust
adults sufficiently to confide in them. If children and young people
do not trust adults in this way, they will, as we have recorded, talk to
no-one. In this case, what confidence should we have in our current
models of and for child protection services? How can we protect
children who can not talk to us? Would more children come forward
if we did not immediately feel morally obliged or legally required to
invoke the mechanisms of 'working together' and to begin the pro-

cess of networking the child's circumstances? It is of interest that amidst all the advocacy of closer inter-agency communication following the events in Cleveland, the lone voice of daycare workers stood out in opposition to this. A unique working context 'based on open ended questioning, developing our children's thinking and trust and offering us many intimate insights into their family life' was transformed, through having to report suspicions of abuse without any discussion with the families concerned, into a situation 'where we were left to face the angry and distressed parents and extended families face to face or by abusive telephone calls, sometimes daily, for weeks on end' (Gilkes 1989, pp.70, 71). Their case was that it was better to have some knowledge and some opportunity to support children in abusing situations than no knowledge at all — for, in their view, the consequence of too much required inter-agency liaison was likely to be a closing down of any communication between families, their children and professionals working in the fields of child care and protection. Parents would stop coming forward to discuss their concerns and worries. We are suggesting that a similar situation may already exist in the case of many children, and that greater adherence to *absolute* promises of confidentiality may be necessary to restore a necessary trust. We return to this point in Chapter 7.

Such a suggestion will be regarded by many as heretical but one is mindful that it is the fate of all truths to begin as blasphemies and to end as superstitions. But we would wish to resurrect a debate which contends that while mechanisms of cross-agency collaboration may be held to be appropriate in the case of those children and young people whose circumstances are palpably dangerous, they may offer little to the far greater number of children and young people who, it seems to us, are likely to continue to suffer in silence. Yet even these children and young people crave straight talking and dispassionate advice based on careful listening to their accounts. This desire is, however, subordinate to their mistrust of adults generally and professionals in particular.

Childline and other phoneline support services

One way around such difficulties is the provision of arms-length and anonymous support services, such as Childline. In all interviews, a tailored question was put to all young people seeking to discover who they might turn to in the event of experiences or anxieties which they felt unable to share with 'confidants' within existing networks of support. Would they prefer an anonymous telephone line or face-to-face discussion with a professional 'stranger'?

The answers were illuminating, if inconclusive. Many young

people said they would on no account shift from their prevailing stance: namely, keep things to themselves, or confide only in best friends, relatives or (occasionally) professionals whom they trusted — 'definitely not. I'd *never* talk to someone who didn't know me about my problems' (girl, 13).

For a minority, in the event of 'no-one else to turn to', Childline (or similar provision like the NSPCC child protection phoneline) was a reassuring back-stop:

> Yeah, I'd ring Childline. I could be honest with them because no-one else would know. They couldn't find out and they [Childline] don't know who they're talking to (girl, 14).

> They'd take you seriously, but they can't see you, so they wouldn't recognise you. I'd use it just to talk but they might be able to help you think about what to do (girl, 13).

Group discussions on this front were revealing and educative in themselves for participating young people. Some individuals had *thought* about ringing Childline but were worried that their parents would find out; they were unaware of the *complete* anonymity of the service to the extent that it did not appear on phone bills. Some children did not realise that they could ring from public call-boxes. One or two had rung Childline not to unload or discuss a problem but 'just to see if it was real' (girl, 12).

Others were more reticent about the likes of Childline, expressing doubts, concerned that they would not know who they were talking to, stating a preference for talking to someone they knew:

> No, I wouldn't. I don't like talking on the phone to someone you don't know. You can't see who you're talking to. They might be laughing at you, although they shouldn't be . . . (girl, 14).

The expression of this vein of thought did not mean that such individuals would more willingly approach a professional 'stranger', although some observed that it would definitely be 'better to talk to a person than a chatline (*sic*)'. They remained, however, cautious in committing themselves on this front because of their entrenched suspicions and anxieties about adult responses and interventions, despite holding clear views about the characteristics and forms of professional support that they would deem to be desirable.

There are times, however, when only a personal contact will do.

Commentary

The almost technical, allegedly 'robotic' nature of professional interventions in children's lives suppress or conceal the more emotional, empathetic level of interaction which children apparently desire, so long as such a response is perceived as personal and genuine. Striking the balance between professional distance and personal affinity is perhaps *the* critical foundation for effective intervention. The issue is one which extends well beyond social work practice with troubled children; it is one which confronts all adult professionals working on a range of substantive themes with children and young people, from drug misuse and criminal justice, to school non-attenders and youth homelessness.

Adults attempting to engage with children and young people need to do so in a different way from adult professionals seeking to support other adults. This is perhaps why organisations such as NAYPIC (the National Association of Young People in Care) have achieved greater success in working with care leavers than more conventional professional programmes and organisations. It is also why there has been a growing interest in peer-led approaches to addressing 'youth questions'. Sixth formers in schools have been enlisted to deal with the problem of bullying in schools; young people have been trained to 'educate' other young people about the risks and dangers of drug misuse and unsafe sex.

The youth service has always asserted that the starting point for any effective work with young people — on any issue — has to be the construction of a positive personal relationship and the building of trust and credibility. Without such a basis, the professional knowledge and skills which are undoubtedly of potential value to troubled young people are useless, since they will be received with suspicion and mistrust. The niceties of social distance and professional detachment are frequently suspended in order to strike up a rapport, and thereby an understanding, with young people. There is no magic recipe for success on this front.

What we are arguing is that the 'personal' must precede the 'technical' for the latter to have any chance of successfully entering the social worlds of children and thereby becoming sufficiently accessible for those young people to make use of. Technical skills are rendered virtually useless if those possessing them lack personal credibility with the children and young people those skills have been designed, developed and finely honed to help. Unlike the carpenter or the bricklayer whose skill-base is paramount and highly visible, and whose personality is largely irrelevant, the effective application of 'helping' skills is, and will remain, heavily contingent upon the personal attributes of the individual who is seeking to make them available to children who apparently need them, but are not necessarily requesting them.

It is these issues that we address in more detail in the next chapter.

5 Professional adults and adult professionals

We have seen in the preceding chapter the deep-seated reticence amongst children about talking to adults. Earlier in the book we drew attention to the range of negative experiences and anxieties, both actual and anticipated, which children routinely encounter. Some, perhaps (and we must always keep in mind the variable 'severity' of such issues in the subjective eyes of children), may not need even the 'listening ear' which an adult might provide. But many are, in some kind of objective sense, indisputably issues which might well benefit from constructive adult intervention and support. What counts as 'constructive' from the perspective of children may be very different from what counts as 'constructive' from an adult viewpoint. Nonetheless, one might seek to argue that, at one level, adults 'know best' for, with the benefit of hindsight and a wider social perspective, adult views are able to place the traumas and anxieties of childhood in a broader context. On the other hand, this is an arrogant claim, for — as we have argued consistently throughout this book — the social world inhabited by children is different from that experienced by an older generation, and adults must be humble enough to acknowledge this and inquisitive enough to be willing to learn about it.

Our folk knowledge of parenting and our anecdotal evidence of the way the likes of teachers and social workers 'steam in' (to use the vernacular of children) to situations in an often completely counter-productive manner bears witness to the fact that, too often, others, the fully paid-up, full-time professional adults of this chapter's title or the adult professionals who often stand in their place, do not 'get it right'.

Children and young people today are simultaneously called upon to work out their own decisions, yet to succumb to adult direction when adults see fit. Increasingly, our research suggests, they endeavour to conceal the problems of their social worlds from adults in order to avoid the latter taking place. One option, clearly, is to let children get on with it, but this is an abdication of our obligations to the younger generation, for it is important for young people to have access to *our* ideas and advice as much as it is important for us to understand their situation. What is *not* called for is the imposition of adult views of the 'older and wiser' variety, for this will simply be rejected by children and young people and cause them to retreat even further into their private worlds which, as we have seen, are often characterised by trauma and anxiety. This chapter examines the type of support and intervention which children and young people say they desire from adults:

> Young people need advice, but not from above by patronising gits. What you want is 'This is what I'd do . . . but it's up to you' (girl, 15).

Children and young people were absolutely clear about what they sought from professionals who purported to be working 'in their interests'. Their arguments were expressed in a variety of ways but certain core and consistent views emerged which, somewhat ironically, did not differ radically from the historically accepted 'principles of social work' first espoused and classified by Biestek (1961).

Listening

Young people want individualised attention — 'not like a robot', as one young woman put it — and careful listening, without trivialising or being dismissive of the issues raised:

> A good listener. Someone who doesn't immediately get back at you with 'oh, you're tired, you'll be all right tomorrow' — that's not listening (girl, 11).

One young man, reflecting on his experience of being taken into care, commented:

> All I ever got was a pat on the head. Nobody ever spoke to me about it — and I'm not one to go to somebody and talk about it. Professionals need to emphasise their willingness to listen and try to understand. If they're willing to listen, I'm willing to tell (boy, 17).

Professionals might, of course, retort that if children are willing to talk then they are willing to listen, but the initiative and effort clearly has to come from both directions and, if at least some young people are so reticent about talking, the greater effort has to be made by those who are professionally charged with the responsibility of supporting them.

Availability

Children and young people also wanted professionals to be available and accessible, something which in their eyes they were not. Even those with current social work support said that contact was not regular or predictable. A commonplace observation was that social workers were 'never there when you want them': 'mine is always out at lunch, off sick, or on a training course' (girl, 15). Young people seeking to divulge their anxieties needed to be sure that relevant individuals would be available — any delay would cause a failure of nerve and, quite probably, an increased reluctance to attempt to forge the link once again.

Non-judgemental and non-directive

Young people additionally wanted professionals to avoid passing judgement on their accounts of their circumstances or behaviour:

> The sort of person who wouldn't say better or worse but just accepted what you said (girl, 13).

This desired non-judgemental attitude was coupled in many children's minds with a non-directive approach in reacting to their depictions of their experiences or concerns: an acceptance of their accounts, however flawed they might be in the context of wider theoretical and social realities. Children wanted 'no pressure' — they wanted patient explanation, the provision of options and suggestions, and the time and space to give them full consideration:

> People offering you support and help but you should always be able to do something different if you want to or if you think it won't work. You don't want to feel you've got to do what they say (boy, 10).

> I want my own choices — otherwise my life might be ruined by someone else's mistakes (girl, 12).

> Instead of saying 'you have to do this', say 'why don't you try this and if you don't like it, don't bother'. People who look at

things from your point of view, who take time to find out what *you're* thinking is best for you (boy, 14).

I think everybody needs advice from time to time but not from people who talk down to you. They should give you choices: 'This is what I'd do, but it's up to you' (girl, 14).

If you're given advice, it should be 'maybe', not 'you must' and they should tell you better why they think something is a good idea (girl, 10).

Most professionals working with children and young people would probably claim that they do endeavour to provide them with choices, yet this is clearly *not* how things are often perceived by children themselves. The imbalance of power between children and adults means that adults must check and check again that children genuinely feel that they are being provided with choices and not being railroaded into certain courses of action. Moreover, the quality of explanation provided by adults (even professional adults), permitting young people to understand why experiences had taken place or problems might be occurring, was often not considered to be satisfactory, according to the young man taken into care at the age of 10:

They said I was too young, that I wouldn't understand. But they never even tried. I was young, but they failed to notice that I was trying to understand. They did things to me — where I lived, where I went to school, the clothes I wore. I always wanted to know *why*. Why did I have to move homes, why did I have to change schools?

All they kept saying to me was that I'd be a 'bright young man' and I'd understand when I was older. What a stupid thing to say. If they thought I was bright, even more so, they should have heard me asking to be told why all this was happening to me. If people refuse to listen and don't even try to explain, it all means nothing. They should have shown more confidence in me, instead of undermining it (boy, 17).

Humour

One should not underestimate the role of humour in effective interaction between children and professionals. A core characteristic frequently mentioned by children related to being 'a good laugh', 'someone you can have a laugh with'. Too many professionals were, in their book, too serious. Children did, of course, want to be taken seriously and the last thing any of them wanted was for professionals to look as if they were laughing *at* them. However, their emphasis on humour suggests that, while they may wish to discuss serious experiences and anxieties with professionals, they want to do so in the context of 'a laugh'. It is clearly a delicate balance to strike and timing is important. Children were certainly hostile to any kind of frivolous attitude but social workers and teachers who were respected were also invariably 'good fun'. Being good fun was certainly no substitute for the other qualities and attributes already mentioned, but it was an important ingredient in the recipe of qualities desired of professionals by young people and one which went a long way in breaking ice and establishing a constructive rapport between them.

Straight talking

Children and young people are usually sharply attuned to the conditions and possibilities in their lives. While they desire professionals to be sympathetic, supportive, optimistic and encouraging, they do not want this to be out of synch with the realities of their prevailing circumstances. They want realism and reliability not, as they sometimes see it, 'bullshit and false promises'. The teachers and social workers who inspired confidence in young people were not always popular, possibly partly because of the advice they imparted:

> *Re: teacher*
> She's prepared to listen to you and she talks straight, not always what you want to hear. But it usually makes sense (girl, 15).

> *Re: residential social worker*
> Everybody complains about her but there's no-one better than her for listening and coming up with good ideas. You don't like admitting it, but she's usually right in the end (girl, 17).

The apparent incompatibility between the desire for someone who is a 'good laugh' and the desire for someone who talks straight even if this makes them unpopular is easily resolved. It is about timing in relation to the compartmentalising of different desirable attributes. In other words, the individual who can be a 'good laugh' in more easy-going and light-hearted moments can also do some tough talking when the going gets serious. Young people don't want superficial friendships with their social workers; they want straightforward and effective support. Too often, they maintain, they get too much effort put into the former at the expense of the latter. And professionals who try to play that 'game' are routinely dismissed as 'dickheads' and a 'waste of space'.

Nor do children want 'false promises'; they want professionals to declare ('come clean') when certain demands are impractical or certain aspirations probably impossible. There is a danger, of course, of adults 'cooling out' such expectations without sufficient justification, but the key issue here is — once again — measured *explanation*. Similarly, when practical support is sought by children and offered by adults, children want tangible delivery. Professionals were systematically pilloried for never keeping their word.

There is, of course, yet again a matter of interpretation which creates a credibility gap between children and professionals. When professionals say they will try, children often assume that they can; when things do not materialise, professionals have 'failed' and children have been 'let down'. Clearer explanation of what is being attempted and its likelihood of success, and more careful checking that children properly understand this, is essential.

Trust and confidentiality

These themes have been held until last, although they are the pivotal issues on which effective and productive communication with professionals takes place. Without them, children will avoid professional arenas of support wherever possible or approach them with caution, doubt and suspicion. Many do already.

It is imperative, *all* children maintained unequivocally, for information shared in confidence with professionals to be treated with *absolute confidentiality*. How then, they were pressed, should professionals deal with the matter if they themselves were unable to help unless they involved other colleagues? Young people were crystal clear about this (which in itself was interesting, given the confusion that often exists amongst professionals themselves about the issue of confidentiality). First, they wanted straight talking — if a professional could not help, they should say so. Second, they wanted consultation — it should be *their* choice if they wanted the matter taken further: 'consult you before spreading things on' (girl, 11). Third, there was always the possibility of professionals discussing the 'problem', anonymously, with other colleagues but, *under no circumstances*, should the individual's identity be divulged or even hinted at, without first securing the consent of the individual concerned. There were no ifs or buts on this front: this was the only way professionals could establish the trust of young people. Sadly, too many young people had direct or anecdotal (not necessarily accurate) accounts of such trust being breached (as we have noted already), causing them to have little confidence in the professional arenas of support which surround them. Confiding in professionals presented too much of a risk: 'you can never be sure'.

So there is incontrovertible evidence that children want and need choices around which to exercise their autonomy and execute *their own decisions*, however much these may have been 'guided' by effective advice and support from professionals. Around the age of 11, they clearly feel capable of making their own decisions and living by their consequences (see Chapter 6). Many have had to already, well before that age. What they definitely do *not* want is to be told what is 'best' for them by others, when it is patently not perceived to be so by them:

> We know what we want — they think they know what we want and try to make us do things their way. But most times, they don't really understand . . . (girl, 14).

It is the failure on the part of not only professionals but also parents and other adults to evaluate what young people are saying and seeking, instead of imposing their own analyses on the presenting situations, which causes so many young people to hold deep reservations about the value of adult support. While we may be arguing to 'humanise' the allegedly robotic styles of professional intervention, we are also stating a case for 'professionalising' the ways in which adults generally respond to the needs and anxieties of children.

Social workers

Many young people do experience problems which, both objectively and subjectively, suggest a need for at least opportunities for support. Many other children and young people have deep anxieties which, again, the opportunity of social work support could potentially alleviate where other mechanisms for support are absent.

However, we have seen already that a substantial minority of young people remain quite adamant that they would not communicate such events to anyone, not even to friends or family, let alone to those within wider professional networks. Furthermore, a considerable number of additional children who do confide in friends or family, or both, stated that they would not discuss their experiences and concerns with professionals such as social workers or teachers, even if their existing networks of support were considered to be inadequate or inappropriate. They hold deep reservations about the quality and effectiveness of adult support.

On the other hand, approaching half (80) of the children and young people to whom we spoke had had some contact with social workers. Young people within the care system clearly had daily contact with residential social workers and routine, if not always regular, contact with field social workers. Thirty-four other children had direct experience of social work intervention for family support or during family breakdown. All children with such direct contact were asked to evaluate their experience of social workers and all other children and young people were probed for their views of social workers, which were invariably gleaned from family 'folklore' or media images, although many of these young people were discerning enough not to 'accept' such images completely at face value.

In these discussions around children and young people's views of social workers, broader but related issues emerged; namely, knowledge and awareness of the Children Act and the 'matching' of social workers to individuals to reflect, for example, gender and ethnicity.

The findings are revealing. There was, without doubt, a prevailing view that social workers could not really provide much in the way of practical value. However, within this rather negative scenario, there was some indication of the potentially valuable support which social workers might deliver, provided they worked extremely hard at breaking down the jaded scepticism which has increasingly permeated young people's perceptions of social workers — and continues to do so.

From direct experience

Negative assessments of social work support and intervention were not always completely damning. Young people often conceded that social workers did try to help, tried to be 'nice' but, ultimately, were incompetent and ineffective. This attitude was epitomised in the crisp summary of her social worker by a 15-year old girl: 'nice person, crap social worker'. The 17-year old, very articulate young man, who has already been quoted frequently, observed:

> I think they've always done what *they* thought was right, but it was based on a sympathy for 'this poor kid'. I never felt they were doing it for me.

This rather instrumental, 'robotic', approach to the social work task was one often repeated by children and young people. Young people routinely alleged that social workers had 'no feeling'.

Criticisms of social workers clustered around four main themes. The first was that they did not listen and therefore did not understand, which in turn meant that they pursued courses of action on their terms rather than through consultation with the young people concerned:

> They're nice, they try to help you, but they don't listen. They

just do things to you. I would like them to listen to me a bit
more (boy, 8).

Social workers don't listen — they're a load of crap. But they
did encourage me to go to school and that's been good for me
(girl, 17).

Nor did they *explain*, resulting sometimes in a complete breakdown
in communication:

They're a load of crap. They don't help. I hardly ever see mine. I
don't know what's happening. They treat me like a little kid, like
a child. They don't think it matters for me to know (boy, 9).

One of the reasons that social workers were perceived not to
listen, explain or understand was that they were disinterested, unre-
liable and not in sufficiently regular contact with young people to
secure a proper grasp of their feelings and their situation. As we shall
see, more positive views of social workers emanated from children
who were regularly 'taken out' by social workers but even this was a
basis for criticism by other young people:

They're basically pen pushers. They bribe kids by taking them
to MacDonalds. They think they make the best decisions for
you when they don't even know you. I've been messed about all
my life by social workers (girl, 14).

Children and young people also felt that social workers made too
many false promises, claiming they would do things but failing to
deliver:

My social worker's a nob, she don't know nothing. She don't
keep promises. She says she'll help you but it's a load of
bullshit. Time drags by and nothing happens (boy, 14).

My social worker's hopeless. He used to promise to sort things
out and said he'd do this and that — but he never did (boy, 14).

They get up your nose. You tell them things and they say they'll
do something about it, but they don't do nothing (boy, 10).

We have, once again, a situation where perceptions may be very
different from realities. No doubt social workers do endeavour to
deliver promises they make: inevitably there will be times when they
are not successful. The issue seems to be that young people may not
be aware of the obstacles which may need to be overcome or even of
the effort which has, in fact, been made on their behalf. Either
'promises' need to be more sensitively rationed or fuller explanation
needs to be given as to why things have not materialised or been
achieved.

Thirdly, there was a lack of faith in the integrity of social workers. They were perceived to break confidences and, as was argued earlier, 'spread things around':

> They distort the truth. They're always telling lies about me to my mum. They look after my mum's interests, not mine. And they always try to involve my family, when I don't want them involved. I just don't trust them. I'd never tell 'em any secrets 'cos they'd just blab it to my mum (girl, 17).

> They always tell someone else — you might not want them to (boy, 14).

> I've valued the social work support here — the care staff treat me nice, respect me. But I don't like my social worker — she's always telling lies about me (girl, 15).

> —   I don't trust her.
> *Interviewer:* Why not?
> —   Dunno. Just got a feeling, she spooks me (girl, 16).

Both the apparent failure to keep promises and this alleged failure to maintain confidentiality leads to the crumbling of any possibility of constructing a trusting relationship. However, the main source of scepticism about social workers was a perception that they were really quite unlikely to be able to do anything anyway:

> I don't want any support from social workers. They're a load of shit. All they do is remind you of what you're like. They're not worth it. What can they do for you, except talk to you? All it is is talking — nothing to do with what's really going on. Just gets you into more trouble — other people contact them to moan about you. They're all talk and no action (boy, 15).

> Their general interest is nice, but they can't really do much for you — you have to get by on your own (boy, 13).

> They lecture you but don't do much else. They don't know nothing. And they talk behind your back (boy, 15).

> I did value social work support when I was younger. Some care staff tried to do their best for us and looked after us. They were around for us. But others have come and gone. They're always moving on. I felt abandoned. They never came back to see us. I've had loads of field social workers. They've all been hopeless. One would start something going, then the next one would start back at square one. They've done nothing for me. They might care but they don't seem to ever get what you want — anything (girl, 17).

My social worker's a div. She does nothing for me. I ask her,
she says 'Yes', but then I don't get it and I never find out why.
They twist your mind round, they confuse you (boy, 15).

They were hopeless — just there. They never did nothing (girl,
13).

Of course, such accusations of 'all talk and no action' may be ill-
founded. Social work practice with children may be substantially
and significantly about *talk* — listening, explaining and trying to
understand, in order to respond positively in the interests of the
child. And some young people did acknowledge these aspects of the
process in a positive way. More often, though, it was the tangible
and visible side of social work intervention which led young people
to hold the most positive views, even if they had been 'bribed' by a
visit to MacDonald's. In many other respects, positive evaluations of
social workers were in essence the upside of the coin whose downside
encapsulated the negative views, thus conveying a sense of what
young people desire from social workers and confirming the characteristics desired by children from adult support which we have
already discussed.

Therefore, despite the greater proportion of negative and critical
observations about social workers, it is important to note that some
young people were emphatically positive about social work support
and intervention. The following exchange took place with a 15-year
old boy:

Interviewer: And what do you think of your social worker?
—   He's all right. He speaks to me and makes me
                laugh. And he gets me involved in activities. The
                social worker before was ace. He used to give me
                money and take me to MacDonald's.
Interviewer: Have they done anything else for you?
—   Can't think of anything else.

An 11-year old boy commented, 'Social workers are all right. They
take you out'.

But it was not all about being 'bribed' with a MacDonald's!
However, the practical support, activities and attention did often,
though not always, seem to be a prerequisite to the establishment of
the foundations necessary for less tangible social work support to
take place and be perceived as effective and valuable:

—   My social worker is brilliant — the best of the lot
                I've had. He takes me out for something to eat and
                helps me when I've got problems.
Interviewer: How does he do that?

— He talks to me about it and then talks to other people (boy, 13).

My social worker is nice. She brought us a birthday present and she looks after us. She tries to do what's best for me (girl, 6).

Other children and young people moved quite directly to compliment social workers around the issues which are their explicit *raison d'etre*:

All my social workers have been good to me — except when they put me in a foster home, and they didn't know it was going to be bad for me. They look after us, care for us, make us laugh (boy, 11).

The one I liked best I had for a long time. She got to know me and I got to know her. We understood each other (boy, 15).

— The social work support has been really good. It's a hard job, but they've been really good. They've helped me through the hard patches. They talk to my mum. I can't. I just argue with her. They're like a bridge between me and my family. I talk to them, they listen. I just want someone to listen and understand what I want to happen.

Interviewer: So what are the most important reasons why you're so pleased with your social workers?

— Keeping promises. They're there when you need them and doing what they say they'll do (girl, 13).

She's nice, she understands me. She listens to me, I trust her. She tries to sort out my problems. She's funny, she makes me laugh. I'd advise her for anyone. I'm very pleased with the support I've had — she's been someone I can turn to (girl, 14).

— They sorted out a lot for me. I didn't really want them involved at first but she's been really good.

Interviewer: What's she done that was really good?

— Just talked. But she was a brilliant person. She really seemed to understand me (girl, 15).

When I was having problems at home, it was good to have a social worker. She saw my point of view. I felt comfortable with her. She helped me to understand what was going on (girl, 14).

Such testimonials to the value of social work support come as something of a surprise — welcome islands in a sea of general negativity and fatalism. At the end of this chapter, some observations will be made as to why there is such polarity in views of social workers who are apparently engaged in the same kinds of tasks with the same 'types' of children and young people.

Some children and young people that we spoke to, notably those who had been in the care system for some time, had experienced a diversity of social work practice. When asked for their views of social workers, they were eager to differentiate between both workers and the issues around which they sought, or were deemed to require, support. In doing so, they reinforced the 'photofit' picture of the characteristics and professional qualities they desired social workers to possess. An 11-year old boy made the following comments:

> *Interviewer:* So what have you made of the social workers you've had?
> — Some have been all right, some have been crap.
> *Interviewer:* What's been the difference?
> — The good ones have been kind to me. They do things quickly once they say they'll do something. They understand how you act and know what's on your mind . . .
> *Interviewer:* And the bad ones?
> — Oh, they never get things done, they're always making promises they never keep.

Others made the following observations:

> Some of them ain't got any time for you. They take their moods out on you. They aren't really interested in anything you're saying. They're always reminding you of the bad things you've done so they don't have to do you any favours. The good ones crash you fags. They give you time when you need it. You can have a laugh with them (boy, 15).

> I can't really remember what any of them have actually *done* for me, but the good ones used to keep in touch with me. They were a laugh, they could take a joke but they were, like, reliable, safe — you could trust them (boy, 15).

> My social worker's a good bloke. Some of them are shit. But I've had mine since I was 10 and he's always happy to come and see me if I need him. I can depend on him (boy, 15).

Second-hand perceptions

> They play a role — a job's a job. They don't really get interested. I bet they never have sleepless nights over the kids they're meant to be helping (girl, 13).

It is worth turning briefly to views of social workers held by children and young people who have never had any direct links with them. Their views emanate from the accounts and comments of friends and family, and from the media, primarily soap operas on TV in which social workers have been portrayed, but also from news bulletins which invariably present social workers in a negative light.

Very few children and young people said that they held no view, possessing insufficient knowledge or images in their head to pass any comment on 'social workers'. The views of other children and young people broadly reflected the diversity of perceptions held by those who did have direct experience of social workers, but they lay more firmly at one end of the spectrum or the other:

They're pompous prats who don't know what they're on about (girl, 14).

They go round knocking on doors asking about children and then they get the police along (boy, 13).

They cause trouble for families. They're always trying to get into people's lives when people don't want them there (girl, 12).

They're a pain in the ass — on the TV, they always hassle you (boy, 14).

They think they know best — but they don't listen. They talk to you but they don't do much (girl, 10).

My parents used to threaten that one of them would come and take me away (girl, 10).

Keep away from them. They interfere. They make unfair decisions. You should scrap 'em — they take kids away from their families (boy, 11).

I wouldn't like to have one — people'd know you'd got a problem (girl, 12).

They're a waste of time — they just go round and round in circles. There's no real solutions anyway. How do they know who's lying and who's telling the truth? (girl, 14).

I wouldn't trust one — they'd tell your parents. That's what they always do (girl, 13).

Like the predominantly negative and suspicious views held by children with direct experience of social workers, these views were also, to some extent, counter-balanced both by purely positive images and by more differentiated observations:

Someone who's friendly who cares about you. Like a nurse —
knows what they're doing (boy, 12).

They're like lawyers. They put things back together again. If it
wasn't for them, where would some kids be?
They listen. They're like a second mother for kids who haven't
really got a mum of their own (boy, 12).
(There was invariably an assumption that social workers were
women.)

They try to help people who've got problems. Like an Agony
Aunt — they sit there and listen and give you advice (girl, 14).

They help kids with problems (boy, 10).

They help a lot. They try to understand. They've got lots of
knowledge about people's problems so they can help to sort
things out by giving you advice and help about it (girl, 13).

It is interesting that few of these children and young people had a
clear idea about the social work task and often characterised social
workers in relation to other jobs which they were able to conceive of
more concretely: nurse, lawyer, agony aunt. Yet there is also a canny
accuracy in such views since social work is, quite centrally, about
caring, advocacy and information and advice.
A handful of more reflective young people sought to make more
qualified comments:

They try to help kids and they work with abusers (*sic*), don't
they? There's lots of negative images about them but they are
there to help and do good (girl, 14).

'Do good' was said here in a purposeful, not a pejorative, way, but
others had doubts as to whether good intentions could be converted
into practical assistance:

I should imagine they're lovely, caring people. The sort of
people you *just might* tell your problems. And they would
probably help if they could, but I don't really think they can do
that much for you except offer useless reassurance (girl, 13).

Whatever their capacity to provide appropriate 'assurance', another
young person argued that social workers were badly portrayed in the
media:

They're meant to help people, aren't they? But you'd never
guess if you watched the telly. On the news, they're always
given a bad name. But they can't all be like that. Some people
must need their help, I should think (boy, 14).

Children's rights and the Children Act 1989

Despite the contradictions and tensions lying just below the surface of the Children Act 1989 (see Freeman 1992), the Act has given explicit emphasis to two specific themes which are of relevance to this chapter. The first is the very limited extension of children's rights to autonomy and self-determination (through consultation and contribution to decision-making, once they are deemed to be 'Gillick-competent').

The second is that all interventions now have to give due consideration to a child's religious, racial, cultural and linguistic background; this includes the provision of social work support by individuals who can and will 'connect' with the background of a child in their care.

Were these issues important to children in our study?

Despite a proliferation of charters and statements informing children of their new rights and responsibilities, even the majority of children in the care system said they knew little about the Children Act (which came into force in October 1991). This finding is consistent with other research such as the Dolphin Project, which found that 'most young people in the project had not heard of the Children Act' (Dolphin Project 1993, p.25).

Those who did have some knowledge of the Children Act held mixed views about the benefits designed to accrue to them:

> Since the Children Act, I think social workers give kids a lot more time. Their effort is more constructively directed — children have got to come first now and we have a right to make demands on them. Yes, it's a good thing (boy, 17).

> The care system has really messed up my life — particularly educationally, with all the school I've missed . . .

> But the Children Act has changed things — now they put us first. Things have changed: the staff have less power, they can't physically control us, and we have access to higher people for advice, if we need it. We can do pretty much what we like.
> That's a problem in a way — everyone in care is just going to be spoilt brats (boy, 13).

> I've missed a lot of school and now I'm getting worried about being able to get a job.
> See, with this Children Act, I can just sit here and do nothing all day. Vegetating — doing nothing. I need to go to school.
> But I don't go, because I know I can get away with it.
> I abuse the situation — it's not doing me any good. They can't

punish me — can't stop my money, can't send you to bed, can't stop you going out, can't do anything. They say it's to save kids from getting institutionalised. So you get everything put on a golden platter for you — that's not life for real, is it? (girl, 14).

They're not allowed to do anything. I go to raves all night and they can't stop me (girl, 16).

Such are the perceptions around the Children Act. During the course of the research — when many children in the care system were watching videos all day instead of going to school, where young people did verbally abuse and challenge residential staff almost mockingly, and where young people did walk out the door at 10.00 pm against the counsel of staff who could do nothing more to stop them — it became very clear that the 'empowerment' of children in the care system had effectively and completely disempowered care staff. Time and again, staff observed that the merest allegation by children against them led to a process of 'suspend first, investigate later'. There was a climate of demoralisation in residential settings of which young people were clearly aware — and they were enjoying every moment of it while it lasted, despite conceding privately that, in the long run, it was doing none of them any favours. More than once, they actually said that a restraining arm was what they needed (even wanted) from time to time — a demonstrable action which showed staffed cared. But care staff could not take the risk in case such action was misconstrued by the child — the ultimate irony, perhaps, given the arguments we have presented earlier.

Young people from Asian, African-Caribbean, mixed race and other minority ethnic backgrounds were asked whether they would prefer a social worker from a similar background to themselves. Only three young people affirmed that this would be a distinct preference. Others maintained that what they wanted was choice. The prevailing view was that, irrespective of race, gender or religion, they wanted a good social worker who would understand. This was summarised by a 14-year old black girl:

Quite honestly, I don't really care what colour they are — I just want a good one.

Whether or not they should be, those children and young people from minority ethnic backgrounds were not particularly preoccupied with their identities, although they were attuned to the possibilities of discriminatory or denigratory practices by racist professionals:

Yes, there are some bad social workers, the sort I'd jump away from. People who look at you differently because of your race.

> I'm part-white, part-Sikh. But I don't practice Sikh religion. Basically, I'm just an ordinary, normal person (boy, 13).

These children and young people were vehemently *opposed* to having social workers of similar backgrounds 'imposed' upon them solely on ethnic or religious criteria:

> My family's from Pakistan but I can't speak, write or read the language. I can't cook Indian food. I know nothing about the culture. Most of my friends are black and reggae is my favourite music.

> They're always giving me Asian social workers who fill my head with shit — why aren't you a good Muslim girl, put Indian clothes on . . . I prefer my jeans and trainers (girl, 17).

Commentary

The key question that needs to be asked is why young people have such mixed, though predominantly negative, views of social workers. To some extent the answer is self-evident. It depends on how far a social worker's characteristics and practice squares with the 'desirable' attributes of an adult confidant, as described in this chapter. And, of course, social workers cannot always 'display' such attributes given their wider professional and legal responsibilities — sometimes they have to 'tell', sometimes they have to take action which is unacceptable to the children concerned.

With these provisos, however, certain observations can be made. The first concerns the *age* of children. Younger children consistently displayed greater faith and confidence in social workers, whether through experience or speculatively: social workers were perceived to provide safety, security and relevant help and support. Secondly, there is the matter of *personality*. There is no doubt that some social workers have a greater ability than others to establish a rapport with young people without compromising their professional role.

Thirdly, there are the issues at play in interactions with social workers. If social workers assist in seeing a way out or finding a way through, their role will be appreciated. If, however, they pursue inappropriate or unacceptable strategies, or fail to resolve the issue of concern (even if it is no more than failure to find a scrambling track on a Saturday afternoon), then they will be vulnerable to criticism and condemnation.

The fourth point is about *'quirkes'* which can — by complete luck and no judgement — make or break initial contact and have implications for the future relationship between a child and a social worker. Favourite football teams, a preference for (or abhorrence of) cheese and onion crisps, the wearing of Doc Martins or the driving of a particular make of car can, by chance, establish an initial line of communication and a fragile credibility from which firmer trust and confidence can flow. The problem is that although such factors may facilitate relationships with some young people (by easing suspicion and providing a platform for conversation) they are equally likely to obstruct the development of relationships with others. Thus it is impossible to plan.

Finally, we return to those themes already discussed hypothetically at the beginning of this chapter and then subsequently largely confirmed through the direct observations of children and young people. Not just listening but being perceived to listen, ensuring that explanations are given and children are consulted, conveying understanding and checking that it synchronises with children's accounts and, where possible, providing children with choices so that they are actively engaged in the ideas and actions that are subsequently pursued — all these themes stand out in children's positive depictions of social workers.

But are children capable of exercising the autonomy and self-determination required to contribute to such a process? Analysts of child development no doubt have a view but, as the next chapter suggests, most children and young people in this study felt that they were already old enough to make rational decisions about their futures.

6 'Safe'

The children and young people whose views are conveyed in this book inhabited a range of personal, social and 'family' contexts. They have contributed experiences, anxieties and opinions derived from very different backgrounds. Across this spectrum, there were the 'survivors', the 'damaged', the 'indifferent' and the 'adaptors', although it would be foolhardy to firmly allocate any individual to any one of these categories. Survival, damage, indifference or adaptation were identifiable as dominant features of their lives but did not necessarily apply to every aspect of it. What was clear was that some children and young people displayed a capacity for thinking through and potentially dealing competently with their predicaments, while others were drifting along in a state of uncertainty, anxiety and confusion. Young people in the care system — many of whom had had the most traumatic childhood experiences — often conveyed a tremendous resilience, almost against the odds, given the situations they were facing:

> — My mum's always drunk too much and she's OD'd a few times. She gets violent and hits me around. Things got really bad when I started going out with my boyfriend. He's black. My mum hates blacks. She kept kicking me out. I ran away and rang the police and they put me on to a social worker. She took me back to mum's but she took my mum's side so I said forget it, packed my stuff and ran away again. I rang the social services and they gave me another social worker. She's brilliant. She really understands me and helps me a lot. I can really *talk* to her. My older sister doesn't want to know me 'cos I've got a 'nigger' boyfriend . . .
> I don't know my dad. I traced him four years ago and telephoned him and he was going to come

over. But we never met. He kept making excuses
— couldn't get a lift, didn't have any money. It's
complicated, because he's got another wife and
another family.

Now my boyfriend won't see me because he knows
my mum doesn't like him. So you see, the worst
thing is rejection by all my family and my
boyfriend. They tell me I'm not part of the family
any more and I'm mature enough to cope. Well
that's true. I've been coping for a long time —
washing, shopping, baby-sitting. I've had to, 'cos
my mum's always drinking. And, whatever they
say, I'm still going to make a life for myself. To
prove to them I can do it. I want to be a nanny and
travel. I think I'll do it: I'm still doing well at
school in spite of everything that's happened.

Interviewer: And how has your 'brilliant' social worker helped?
—   Oh, she's great. I see her regularly and she even
comes down to my school to explain things, if I ask
her to. It's just something about her. She's really
nice. She seems to know what I'm thinking. And
she stands up to my mum. Not many people would
do that (girl, 15).

This resilient and gritty determination to 'make a go of things' was
not commonplace. Nor, as we have seen, were such positive ap-
praisals of social work support. More often, children presented an
abject fatalism that little could be done by them, let alone others, to
stem the tide of negative experiences or persistent anxieties. You just
do what you can to alleviate, mitigate or avoid the worst: 'look after
your back and sod the world' (boy, 13).

We have recorded the range of 'worst experiences' and major
'anticipated anxieties' conveyed by the children and young people
interviewed. Although, clearly, these do need to be mediated by
professional interpretation and analysis, they must also be received
as authentic and important, if represented by children as significant.
A central criticism made by children of professional responses is that
they are not treated 'seriously'. However 'trivial' such issues may be
in the spectrum of potentially damaging experiences, they are important to *them*. So, to paraphrase an earlier quotation, if children
are willing to tell, adults must be willing to listen.

That, of course, pre-supposes that children are willing to *tell*.
What has emerged from our research is the strength of non-professional networks of support, located largely around the family, in
whom children confide. Many who benefit from such networks

would not dream of turning further afield for support, advice and intervention. There is an implicit policy suggestion here, that perhaps professional support services should give serious consideration to making themselves more accessible to the adults in whom children do place their trust, in order for them to dispense accurate guidance and support. Perhaps future research should consider exploring the views of these 'significant others' about their confidence and capacity to provide appropriate choices and information.

What has also emerged from the research we conducted is that a substantial number of children and young people have no confidence whatsoever in adult support of any kind. They talk to 'no-one'. The reasons for this turn on a number of related issues. Many children are adamant that there are no solutions, but believe there could be a lot more understanding. This 'understanding' is both about taking them seriously and about accepting *why* they are seeking to divulge their experiences or anxieties.

We have drawn attention to the three reasons why young people may communicate their experiences and worries to others. The most common — flowing from the pervasive belief that little can be done to actually change things — is to 'get things off your chest'. Young people simply want to unload their troubles on a listening ear:

> I only talk to people to get things off my chest so you don't get even more clogged and more worried (boy, 10).

There may, perhaps, be an implicit quest for choices which might possibly effect change although, as stated, there is often an overriding assumption that efforts to effect change will be futile. However, secondly, children talk in order to seek advice and actively explore the choices open to them. They do not want to be 'disempowered' by others taking action; they want to know the range of options available. Equipped with this information, they will then make up their own minds about which course of action to take. It may not necessarily be the 'right' one in professional terms, but it will be the right one for them at the time — and, if it is 'wrong', they will have to learn from their mistakes. The children and young people we spoke to were powerful advocates of the need for 'experiential learning'.

Thirdly, there are times when young people are seeking more than advice and information, when they are hoping to enlist support, direction and action by others. When this is the case — and careful checking is required to be sure that this is what they want — it is critical that adults present a realistic picture of the possibilities, otherwise children will have been victim to yet more false promises and raised expectations.

These three themes are, of course, 'ideal types' which in reality blend into one another. Professionals, and other adults, endeavouring to assist children with their difficulties are operating on shifting sands, for a child's 'agenda' may alter as an account unfolds: their responsibility is therefore to *check constantly* what that 'agenda' is — *how* does the child want them to respond?

Even if they in fact seek advice and direction (on the grounds of not feeling 'adult' enough to make autonomous decisions), this is rarely likely to be admitted. The testimony of the child who quietly conceded how apposite much parental direction was, but would not openly acknowledge this, bears witness to this point:

> Sometimes your parents do know best. It's not what they say, it's how they say it. You feel they're pushing you to do things. I think I know what's best for me, but a lot of the time I do follow my parents' advice, even if I pretend I'm not going to! (girl, 13).

This notwithstanding, many children and young people believe they can be, or circumstances force them to be, responsible for their own decisions and are resistant to being told what to do and to others doing things for them, without consultation, even if this is premised upon it being in their 'best interests'.

As a result, their primary desire is for the provision of relevant and (to them) sensible choices, because it is they who, ultimately, will have to live by the choices they make. We emphasise the idea of relevant and appropriate choices. Children and young people frequently felt that the choices presented by adults were unworkable in 'real life' — whether going to the police about being raped ('even if he goes to prison, he'll get out sooner or later and then he'll be after us; hopefully, he'll go down for something else' — girl, 15), or a parent having a word with the head teacher of a school over a case of bullying. It is the young people who will have to face the consequences of what are considered to be 'appropriate' solutions by adults but inappropriate to children.

The question of autonomy

Whatever the level of aspiration amongst children to exercise autonomy and choice, many parents and professionals would maintain that children (and even 'young people') are not yet ready or capable to make independent decisions from a free range of choices. Even the concept of Gillick-competence, enshrined in the Children Act 1989, which requires that children can show sufficient knowledge and understanding of their situation before they can be permitted some sense of self-determination, begs all kinds of definitional questions.

Guidance and, if necessary, direction is, according to adult wisdom, still often required. The potentially damaging effects of the 'freedom' allotted to children in the care system under the Children Act has already been alluded to, in comments made by some children, earlier in this book. We turn here to examine what other children interviewed had to say about the question of autonomy, prompted by a 'devil's advocate' question along the lines of 'but surely you're not yet old enough to make your own decisions?'.

With the exception of the small group of Asian young women and a handful of other children and young people, there was a strong consensus that the capacity and *right* to self-determination materialised on the threshold of transition from top juniors to secondary school. This was generally agreed to be the 'watershed', although some children and young people — particularly those in the care system — maintained that they should be (or should have been) allowed to make their own decisions even younger:

— I think kids should be given the freedom to make their own decisions, although adults should help them think about the choices available.

Interviewer: But *when* should this be — at age 7, or 10, or 14, or what?

— From the first year in high school. When you go to high school, you're no longer mollycoddled in cotton wool. You've got to stand on your own feet (girl, 14).

A group of 13-year olds also argued forcefully for the provision of options:

— What you want is a good friendly ear, someone who listens . . .

— . . . not teachers who say you're pathetic and don't want to be bothered with little kids' problems . . .

Interviewer: But are you 'little kids' who need telling what to do?

— No way. There's things we don't know about, sure, but we can make our own decisions. We have to.

Interviewer: And how long have you been able to do that?

— Since we came to this school. Before that, you're only little and your parents and teachers look after you.

Interviewer: And they don't now?

—   We can look after ourselves. We just need people
          to help us think things through.

This self-assurance was at times qualified in different ways. One
14-year old boy, when asked about his capacity to make his own
decisions, commented:

Since I've been at secondary school. Even before that I used to
think I knew, but now I know that's not true.

More ambivalent young people still believed, for pragmatic
rather than more idealistic reasons, that they had to learn to exercise
autonomy, even if they were unsure of the extent to which they were
capable of making, and living by, their own decisions:

Not really. We're children rather than young adults. But we
still have to learn for ourselves. Adults won't help us (boy, 13).

Sometimes we know what to do, sometimes not. We should
listen to adults and think about what they say but then we
should be allowed to make our own choices. We've got to learn
to do that sometime anyway (girl, 11).

A theme running through this whole book is the message that
children believe that, like it or not, *only they* can sort things out for
themselves. The crisp response of one individual, when asked about
autonomy, was 'Yes, you've got to be' (girl, 9). This apparent fatalism was coupled with a powerful advocacy of 'experiential learning'
— only through giving children responsibility for their own decisions, and allowing them to learn from their mistakes, could they
establish their independence and autonomy:

Interviewer: Do you feel confident and knowledgeable enough
          to make your own decisions?
—   Yes, for most things. I can look after myself. I
          need adult guidance to find things out. I trust
          adults to give me information, but not to solve my
          problems for me. You have to do that for yourself
          (girl, 10).

—   Yes, I feel confident and grown-up. The basic
          problem is always thinking the grass is greener on
          the other side. No-one really knows and only you
          can find out (girl, 15).

—   At the end of the day, it's up to us. We have to
          learn from what we've done. We have to learn from
          our mistakes. You can't rely on your parents

forever. We have to be allowed to make our own
choices and find out for ourselves (girl, 13).

What is being conveyed here seems to be quite clear. Children
and young people experiencing difficulties and anxieties want adults
to provide them with ideas and information on which they can make
informed choices (which, of course, may still not necessarily be the
'right' ones). They want to feel that they have actively influenced
and directed the courses they are taking in their lives. Regrettably,
as we have seen, their perception that adults do not respond in this
way, and tend to consign them to the role of passive recipients of
adults' decisions, makes them wary of placing their trust and confidence in others. In this way, they retain control, but the price they
pay is to have to make their own decisions on what can often be
limited choices and misguided information.

There is, then, a general thread of argument emanating from the
research we undertook. For the majority of children and young
people, almost irrespective of circumstances, the world is a place in
which they must learn to cope alone. Either they mistrust adults *per
se* or they mistrust the actions they may take. As a result, they retreat
to a position where problems are shared not to be solved, but to be
unloaded. The unloading of problems takes place primarily with
'best friends'. Where young people do seek advice and choices, they
usually confide in particular individuals within their extended family
whom, for a variety of reasons, they trust and whose ideas they
respect. Even in the absence of such support from relatives, there is
a deep reluctance to communicate concerns to any adults, professional or otherwise, beyond the family circle. And a substantial
minority are reticent about sharing their experiences and anxieties
with anyone.

Nonetheless, many children and young people had had some
quite traumatic experiences and most had private anxieties which
caused them deep concern, despite the massive gulf between the real
negative experiences of some young people and the anticipated worst
experiences of many others. 'Ordinary' children were quite
incapable of even imagining the kinds of harmful situations which
had actually been experienced by some of their contemporaries.

The most prevalent negative experiences clustered around the
two key locations in children's lives: family and school. Bullying and
name-calling at school were recurrent experiences for a substantial
number of children, as were family arguments, and sometimes
violence and abuse in the home. It is important to note that it was
not always the presenting experience itself, but the sequence of
events which followed it, which proved to be most traumatic for the
children concerned.

Central anxieties experienced by children and young people also clustered around worries about family friction, separation and death, and bullying at school. A third key area of anxiety expressed by teenage girls was the fear of sexual harassment and assault and an accompanying fear of 'looking stupid' or over-reaction by parents and other adults if they expressed such concerns to them.

Whatever the nature of the experience or anxiety, children and young people had clear ideas about what kind of support they desired — which invariably incorporated a role for them in contributing to the formulation of any 'action' which might be considered, as well as describing their concerns — and about the central characteristics required of adults (and, indeed, friends) before they invested their trust in them. The widespread perception was that adults generally, and professionals in particular, did not meet such aspirations. Adults appeared to them to possess a world-view which was quite out of step with their own. As a result, they were perceived to fail to listen, to misinterpret the messages being conveyed and, consequently, to trivialise, dismiss or over-react.

The reasons some children did express confidence in some adults, including some professionals, do not lend themselves easily to rational analysis. Frequently they are unfathomable, based on an empathetic belief that a particular adult (whether an aunt or a social worker) is 'safe'. At other times, they are a product almost of a 'lucky break' — resulting from appearance or a comment which connected fortuitously with a child's cultural (in its broadest sense) preferences or, sometimes crucially, with their sense of humour. Time and again, the most favoured adult support revolved around some serious listening inside a funny shell. Young people's lives are routinely about backchat, sharp remarks and flippant asides, often all the more so amongst those experiencing difficult childhoods. The 'best' social workers were often *first* described as those who make them laugh, *then* as those who listen.

It is such 'maverick' qualities — which hardly lend themselves to professional training, planning, preparation or development — which underscore successful supportive relationships with children and young people. Only then can the more formal 'professional' qualities — which can be acquired and developed through training and practice — be added: listening, explaining, being non-judgemental, confidentiality, consultation. Only then will such attributes strike the chord necessary to cement effective and supportive professional interventions.

This is bad news for those who are responsible for providing advice, support and information for children and young people. But the general message is, if not bad news, riddled with contradictions. Even when children do talk to adults, they rarely convey the whole truth. Many interviews included a provocative question by the researcher along the lines of 'but if you only tell half-truths, how do you expect accurate or appropriate responses to your wishes, needs or aspirations?' Children and young people commonly conveyed the 'vulnerability' they believed would accrue if they 'came clean' or bared their soul. If all was divulged, disempowerment (or the perception of it) was complete. Basically, adults could not and should not be trusted with a full account of a situation because children had no idea how they would respond to it. It is a classic Catch-22. Likewise, although children were quick to condemn adult interventions, a lack of interest or intervention was equally condemned, because it conveyed an impression of not caring. The paradox, then, is that whatever adults do, the odds are that it will be subject to criticism. If they don't intervene, they don't care. If they do intervene, their reactions are inappropriate. Although children only tell segments of a story, they expect adults' responses to be as if they knew the whole of it.

It might be alleged, then, that children want to have their cake and eat it — that it is they who seek a 'golden platter' world. But in fact the reverse is much more true. Children, generally quite realistically, feel that they have little power to exercise influence over their lives. They believe that they can and should be allowed far greater autonomy — following discussion and consultation with trustworthy adults — over what happens to them. By and large, however, they are fatalistic that things will take their course and that there is not much they can do about it. They can only hope that 'worst-case' scenarios will not materialise, or be repeated, for them. Nevertheless, they do seek advice and information which may help them to think through and devise their own strategies for overcoming or avoiding the more troubling episodes in their lives.

From the evidence presented in this unashamedly one-sided account of children's views, those adults and professionals responsible for providing such support are patently failing to deliver. Their task is, even children would admit, by no means an easy one, but it is one that is critical to ensuring that children do act, and are supported in acting, on accurate and relevant information. Children are only too eager to know the likely consequences of different courses of action before they take one. The weight of evidence which flows from our analysis is that children do need (as well as want) choices, and it is only adults and professionals committed to their welfare and development who can provide them. But, from the point of view of children and young people, there is still much to be done to construct and re-establish the trust and confidence which will allow them to receive it in the spirit in which it is delivered.

The essential question is whether the adult world wants to assist children in feeling 'safe' (as *children* define it) or to ensure that children appear to be 'protected' (as adults define it). The former demands flexible, sensitive interventions along the lines of those described by the children whose voices can be heard in this book. These will require adults to respect and keep the confidence and confidentiality of children and young people to a far greater extent than they are used to doing; it will require adults to countenance much more self determination by children and young people which may be experienced as taking even greater risks; it will require greater trust and faith than either party would currently seem to have in and for the other. The latter form of intervention calls for rigid procedures imposed from above in response to political and professional imperatives, where it is the adult who feels safe from the uncertainties of an uncertain world and the hostility of an unforgiving public and press. The latter may satisfy the 'social conscience' but only the former can enable children and young people to equip themselves with the resources to deal with the social realities they currently encounter or expect to encounter in the future. It is therefore this task which should provide the driving force for social work endeavour, underpinned by the value-base of meeting individual needs; for without such a value-base, social work practice is vulnerable to blowing around in the political wind (Lorenz 1993) with no anchor point to ensure it is grounded in the real lives and hopes of those it seeks to serve.

The next chapter explores how such an approach might be operated in practice.

7 '... and well?'

This Chapter was written by Neil Hopkins, Head of Children's Services, NSPCC Cymru/Wales and the Midlands with Ian Butler and Howard Williamson.

Introduction

We believe that, arising out of the material that has been presented in this book, there are implications for practitioners and service planners across a wide range of professional activities that involve direct work with children. Our specific interest is in the field of child protection and it is to a consideration of practice in this area that we now turn.

We have already made some observations on the nature of abuse and the (essentially adult) construction of 'child protection' (Chapter 3). In Chapter 6, we developed the idea of what children might mean when they use 'safe' to describe both people in whom they can have trust and situations in which they might seek help and or support. In this chapter we attempt to reconcile the terms 'protected' and 'safe' in such a way that does not distort either.

We have no difficulties whatsoever in supporting the actions of adults taken to protect any child or young person in imminent and unequivocal risk of significant harm. Nor, one imagines, does anyone else. The problem arises in the fact that there are as few 'smoking guns' in child abuse as there are in any other sphere of human activity. The 'facts' are more often in dispute and both the motivation of the perpetrator and the consequences for the victim more difficult to determine with any degree of precision. Nonetheless, we do not intend to imply any significant conflicts of either interest or expectations between adults and children in the matter of what makes a child safe or protected. What we do suggest is that in the continuing negotiation around what constitutes abuse and what should be considered as an appropriate response, a sharper ear should be turned to what children and young people have to say on the subject so that an even stronger and more effective model for practice can emerge.

To further that end, we have attempted to extract certain 'principles' that, we feel, reflect broad themes that run through much of what young people have been saying to us and have then sought to relate these to key aspects of practice and planning in the sphere of child protection. For many, this will simply reflect existing good practice and, in applying these 'principles for practice', we will be having regard to those principles already established in child protection agencies' standards and procedures, especially where these have been reinforced by the views of the young people with whom we have spoken. However, we will also, inevitably, be raising some challenges to other established principles that may pose certain difficulties for professionals enmeshed within the current legal and policy framework and form the basis of further debate.

I   Working with children who have had traumatic experiences

Principle:
When working with children who have experienced abuse, it is vitally necessary to establish what children themselves see as the primary causes of pain, distress and fear.

In child protection work, it is clear that designing relevant responses to the needs of young people who have been harmed depends on the social worker or other professional agency having an accurate and realistic understanding of the child's problem. A process of problem definition that fails to take into account what the child's own priorities are, as well as the circumstantial or other 'objective facts' of the case, is likely to result, at best, in ineffective strategies to improve children's lives and, at worst, to professional responses that are themselves abusive to children.

Such a proposition does not follow automatically from current guidelines on assessment and the process of problem definition and action planning. Successive reports and guidance from the Department of Health (DOH 1988, HO/DOH 1991, DOH 1991a) place great emphasis on the need for more efficient communication between agencies and the families they work with; on greater effectiveness in inter-agency working and on the importance of structure and planning in child protection work. The need for practitioners to develop meaningful partnerships between parents/carers and professionals is widely advocated. So too is a more systematic approach to information gathering and decision-making and for the need for clearer procedures that, in turn, support clarity of role and responsibility of individual professionals. However, noticeably little is made of the child or young person's role as being 'expert on themselves'.

There is little mention of the need to talk and listen to the child or young person to establish what their specific needs and priorities are. In other words, there is no strong sense of the importance of establishing what aspect of their particular problem it is that the child or young person wishes to address.

If, as professionals, we are unable to take time to discover what it is that most concerns or frightens children about their circumstances, including our own impact on them, it should not surprise us if their response to our efforts to help them is one of confusion, mistrust and defensiveness.

In cases of serious and unequivocal abuse of children, for example, where the abuser is one or both parents, our adult/professional definition of a child's real priorities are often for him or her to be in a 'safe place', away from their home and parents, while action is taken to either lessen the nature of any future risk and/or to mediate the effects of the abuse. This will almost certainly be the correct and responsible view for the professional to take, but the process that leads on from such responses will be improved if those carrying them forward are aware of the individual child's own chief concerns.

These might be, for example, 'I cannot be away from my younger brother and sister' or 'last time I was in care the other children bullied me and I never saw my social worker until I was ready to return home'. Such concerns are also of vital importance if the child is to feel safe as well as to be protected.

Inability to hear what children are saying can and does create further fear and distress to add to that already caused by the experience of abuse and we must recognise that for some, at least, the harm does not stop when the helping starts. We contend that it is imperative to keep checking and you will be perceived as 'safe' as well as protecting.

Principle:
Children's perceptions and fears, as well as acknowledged traumatic events, can have a significant impact on children's lives and wellbeing and these need to be addressed and validated at all stages of investigation, assessment and therapeutic work.

In a sense, this principle is the justification for the previous one but bears separate re-statement. Professionals working in agencies

under tight budgetary constraints, with heavy workloads and subject
to unnecessarily mechanistic legal systems and inter-agency procedures may understandably take the view that they cannot afford to
go looking for imaginary problems that children might anticipate or
to begin work on issues that are of less importance, at least to them
as adults.

It is difficult enough to design services that respond to children
whose trauma is backed up by 'hard' evidence that can be understood and accommodated by our legal systems and child protection
procedures. However, the distress and damage that can be caused by
children's worst anticipated experiences is very real for the child
and, if not recognised, may lead to his or her recovery being significantly impaired. We have recorded already the very striking observation of one young person who has been reassured that the perpetrator of the abuse that she suffered will not return but who told us
that he comes back every night, in her dreams.

Children who have been abused and who are in the child protection system will have experienced dramatic shifts in their circumstances with the accompanying feelings of uncertainty about their
present and their future that go with dramatic change. In planning
work with young people who have been placed on child protection
registers or who are being looked after in residential or foster care, it
is all the more important to address the real fears that children may
have about their current circumstances or their short and long term
futures.

At a wider level, we may have to review our professional priorities in terms of what constitutes the kind of harm to children that
warrants a systematic and strategic response by child care professionals and adults more generally. We, and many others before us
have drawn particular attention to the issue of bullying, for example:

Principle:
*Child care practitioners should actively address the consequences and
associated difficulties resulting from traumatic events experienced by
children and pay special attention to the effects of those actions taken
specifically to protect the child.*

Young people who have experienced abuse are more likely to
have problems within their future relationships with adults and with
other children, including their own (see Bolton, Morris and
Maceachron 1989, pp. 71–2). They are at higher risk of becoming
involved in drug and other crime-related activities (see, for example,
Takii 1992, Dembo *et al.* 1992).

This may, in part, be explained by the psychological and
emotional consequences of the abuse itself. It is self-evident that to
address the child's needs and priorities, it is important to include a

detailed and broad assessment of the medium and longer term consequences which may result from the incident(s) of abuse themselves.
An overly narrow focus on the more tangible and visible signs of
abuse can fail to address the needs of the 'whole child' which can,
itself, result in more severe risk or damage than the original inci-
dent(s) of abuse.

It may, in part, be explained also, by the routine effects of the
'care system' (DOH 1991c, DHSS 1985). In part too, it may be
explained by the way in which child protection services deny any
significant role, other than victim, to the children or young people
themselves.

Attention needs to be paid too to the demoralising and de-skilling
consequences of ill informed, child-saving zealots who, in their
eagerness to rescue the child, render them powerless to direct any
part of their recovery or even claim their part in it from that point
on. Sections II and III of this chapter consider some ways in which
children and young people may play a more prominent part in their
own protection.

II   Who children want to work with

Principle:
*Children should always be consulted, as part of the negotiation and
review of work, to identify any preference they may have regarding
the gender, race and culture of their worker.*

In the 'real' world, resources may well limit the choices that
children have in relation to the gender, race or culture of those
working with them. Children may also have alternative criteria about
who they would most like to work with them, i.e. a 'sense of
humour' or an optimum age, perhaps even something to do with
'style'. These may sound to many adults unimportant, even irrelevant, qualities on which to base a choice of worker. This may
ultimately be so, but it is equally important not to ignore or automatically rule out any preference put forward by children. They may
relate to an experience that the child has had that the worker is
unaware of.

We should not lose sight of the fact that the act of negotiation
itself is an opportunity for professionals to show that they take the
young person and what they say seriously. It also gives the worker an
opportunity to engage with the child early on in the work on a
subject that is a familiar and welcome topic of conversation — his or
her likes and dislikes!

If the young person's choice is not available then the practitioner should give him or her clear and honest feedback about the reasons for this and an account of the efforts made to identify someone who might fit the child or young person's stated preference.

Principle:
Children should always be consulted, as a formal part of any individual programme of work, on their choice of 'safe' or 'trusted person' to support them.

It is clear from children's accounts that their choice of 'safe' or trusted person to assist them through the investigation, assessment or recovery process, may not necessarily be the key professional assigned to manage or deliver the social work or other services. It would be surprising if this were the case. What is not surprising is that young people do need someone or something that is special to them, that they can rely on and confide in, especially during periods of fear, uncertainty and loss.

Children's choice of trusted person is a particularly important and intimate one, especially for an abused child whose trust in her/his carers and family may have been misplaced and betrayed in the past.

The role of the trusted persons re-emphasises the importance of establishing significant people in the child's network in child protection work. This will give clues about who the child sees as safest or most helpful to them in their day-to-day lives. To take this a stage further, it may be appropriate in some cases to 'de-professionalise' the service to children by putting the trusted person in charge of working with them, with the professional supporting and supervising the work.

Child protection procedures would not allow this approach in most authorities on the grounds that it would constitute unacceptable risks to a child to have a non-professional as their 'key worker'. Certainly such an alternative method of working would involve professionals, particularly field social workers, giving up a significant amount of control to whoever the child chooses as trusted person. There remains the possibility that their choice may be impractical at best or, at worst, be someone who presents a clear risk to the child that social workers are unaware of or unwilling to accept. Yet it is already being suggested that key components of the field social worker's role should be delegated to residential staff, for example, who often 'received a better press from the young people than field social workers' (Buchanan 1994, p.34). If this practice were widely accepted then, as a principle, the dominance of the field social worker would be broken and the prospect of other patterns of service delivery made more likely.

Principle:
*In allocating and planning work, priority should be given to
ensuring continuity of key practitioners/trusted persons.*

Young people have stated their need for continuity of persons
who provide them services. The need to change key workers in child
protection cases may well occur for operational reasons which make
sense to individual professionals or their team/agency or the child
protection case conference. However, from what young people have
told us, this does have a significant and unsettling effect on the child
concerned. It can further reinforce the levels of uncertainty that
children are experiencing and can detrimentally effect the degree of
trust that young people are willing or able to place in professionals
and other adults in the future. After all, in their eyes, they may
already believe that the professional's interest in them is 'just a job'.

If there is a change in key worker, every effort must be made to
manage the transition so that it is sensitive to the young person's
needs for information and to have their feelings heard and acknowledged. If professionals are not able to adopt this planned and sensitive approach marking the significance of this transition for the
child, then the child's ability to make healthy relationships with
other practitioners may suffer and with it their ability to move on
and grow.

Operational planning should, therefore, aim to achieve maximum continuity of key worker for each child who is receiving the
service as a standard of good practice.

Part III   Trust, involvement and confidentiality

Principle:
*When receiving information from children about their concerns,
practitioners/workers should make quite sure that they understand
why children are sharing the information and what form of help they
require.*

Children give, as one of their chief reasons for not sharing information with adults, their fear that the adult will take the problem
from them, giving their own interpretation to the young person's
account and responding in ways that fit their own perceptions and
concerns. In child protection work professionals are expected and
encouraged to clarify factual information where there are concerns
about children and to act in their interests without unnecessary
delay. These are important principles of good practice, but it is
equally important to adopt a planned and considered approach in

our work with children that includes what it is the child wants to see in our response.

Failure by the child care professional to take into account why the young person has shared information and contacted them for help, may result in the professional having a distorted view of what the child or young person's real priorities are. This, in turn, may result in the professional responding in ways that are not perceived as helpful by the child which will influence the likelihood (the *lesser* likelihood) of their sharing concerns in the future.

Principle:
Working agreements with young people should ensure that they retain maximum possible choice/autonomy within the working relationship, while having easy access to advice and support outside of it.

Consistent with the theme of 'giving the young person the right to be an expert on her/himself' and not taking children's problems away from them, professionals should develop joint working agreements with children that respect their individuality and rights to choose what they wish to achieve and how they wish to achieve it. This should be a realistic contract based on the 'real world' of the child and the professional and should be set in the context of the professional's responsibility to protect the child from significant harm.

Young people are telling us that they value and respect appropriate limits placed on them but that they, in turn, need to find their own solutions with support of other children, trusted persons and professionals.

Principle:
Upon receipt of information from a child about her/himself, practitioners/workers should always consult the young person about their mandate to take action and about the form and content of any such action.

Principle:
Clear and understandable 'confidentiality contracts' should form part of all work agreements and reviews.

At the heart of any discussion of child protection work is the question of risk, usually that associated with the potential for future harm to the child. There is a sense in which extending the notion of the rights of children and young people to confidentiality and to direct more actively the course of any particular intervention, may be felt, inevitably, to increase that risk. 'Guilty knowledge' held by the worker, derived in confidence and with a prohibition on its use, cannot be a mandate for future, protective action, not without, at the

very least, some anguish on the part of the professional and considerable damage to any working relationships with the child.

Associated with a determination to protect the child however,
may be a certain, quite reasonable inclination to protect oneself,
professionally and psychologically from the consequences of inaction
in the face of prior knowledge. Given such powerful incentives to
limit the boundaries of confidentiality between the child and the
worker and to retain overall, if not absolute, control over events, it is
difficult to accept that this all too familiar approach also carries risk.
There is substantial risk generated in the lives of young people who
have told us that they will talk to no-one about what worries or
harms them because they do not believe that adults are able to
understand them. There is substantial risk in those situations where
young people's experience of adults is that they 'blab' such that they
no longer trust them with the things that really matter. And there is
real risk that an agenda that is wholly constructed by the adult will
cause as much harm in the long term as it will avoid in the short
term.

This shift in the boundaries between confidentiality, autonomy
and the central role of the adult is recognised to some degree by
the development of confidential telephone services for children,
although these do not receive unqualified support from the young
people with whom we spoke. Our view is that child protection
professionals should be prepared and supported adequately to accept
a higher degree of risk, certainly professionally and psychologically,
than might at first seem comfortable or familiar in order that children and young people will regard them as 'safe'. Only in this way
can the professional go on to ensure that the child remains protected.
It is difficult to envisage how one protects a child who neither trusts
you, respects you or even speaks to you.

This can be managed, formally, to some degree, by the use of
'confidentiality contracts' established at the outset of any piece of
work. Such a formal negotiation with the young person as to which
pieces of information can be used for what purposes will reinforce to
children the message that there is respect for their autonomy and
remind the worker that there is a trade-off between confidentiality
and risk.

IV   Planning and engagement

Principle:
In planning work, children should understand and be involved in

*setting objectives/timescales which should be realistic, achievable
and have meaning/relevance for the young person.*

The importance of a formal engagement process in all work with
children cannot be overstated. It is an invaluable opportunity for
initial relationship building with the young person. A 'getting-to-
know' and familiarisation time during which questions can be responded to, initial fears, anxieties and misunderstandings addressed,
and when the young person can put their stamp on the shape and
nature of the work.

Principle:
*Work plans/agreements should include a section dedicated to
individual children's definition of their problems and the effects that
these are having on them.*

To help ensure that the young person's viewpoint is properly
valued and reflected in the work, all workplans should include a
section dedicated to the child's description of their problems and
concerns which should be reviewed throughout the work.

The child's problem definition should be included in any final
report or assessment of the piece of work as one important measure-
ment of how successful the work has been from the child's or young
person's point of view.

V   What children require from practitioners/trusted persons

Principle:
*Practitioners/trusted persons should have the ability to listen to and
understand what individual children require and have the skills to
design specific programmes of work to meet their different needs.*

This principle relates to the skill and competence levels of child
care professionals involved in child protection work. It addresses the
need for local authority and voluntary sector field and care workers;
health workers; the police; teachers; and lawyers to have skills in
communicating with children, particularly those who have been
traumatised, through access to relevant training and to quality
supervision and management of their practice.

We believe that we have given some indications already (Chapter
2) of what the essential skills of listening to children might imply but
would repeat at this point that the primary pre-requisite is a
preparedness to listen and be informed.

Principle:
Practitioners/trusted persons should ensure that all young people with whom they are working should have the ability to contact them in person when they wish/need to do so.

This principle presents similar difficulties to that of providing maximum continuity of worker for children in that it relates to agencies' finite and limited resources as well as the needs of professionals to be away from their work and to live a life that does not include their clients having unlimited access to them.

One arrangement that would meet the needs of children who need to contact their key worker in an emergency, would be to identify another professional, who may or may not work in the same agency, or someone in the child's community who s/he would identify as a trusted person as an alternative contact point when the key worker is not available. Child abuse does not keep office hours so neither can child protection services. This is not to say that existing services should spread themselves ever more thinly but it is to suggest that where comprehensive services do not exist, one priority for professionals should be the development of such a network, possibly using existing community resources.

Principle:
Practitioners/trusted persons should ensure that children are aware of/understand the options available to them during the professional's or other adult's involvement with them.

Children confirmed to us their interest in understanding the options available to them so that they had a clearer view of their possible futures and so that they would be in a better position to make informed choices. This principle is already recognised by most agencies working with children and is incorporated within their practice standards and procedures.

Principle:
Practitioners/trusted persons will provide children with information about services that is relevant to their needs, readily understandable and factually correct.

The young people we spoke to stressed the importance they placed on having available to them as much information about services as possible. This was particularly important to children who are engaged with child protection services and procedures, the process of which can be complex and confusing. One consequence of the development of a multi-agency approach to working with children at risk of significant harm is that there is greater potential for children to misunderstand professionals' different roles and responsibilities.

Accessible information that explains the work process, who is involved and what their specific roles are, and clearly stating what the child's rights and responsibilities are, will assist children by decreasing the potential for confusion and misunderstanding that is so often a part of child protection work.

Principle:
Children's perception about the reliability and effectiveness of services/service providers should be recorded and addressed in service evaluation and practice supervision.

To ensure that design and planning of children's services takes into account the service-users' need to make choices, all agencies providing services to young people should include in their evaluation of the effectiveness of their work, routine monitoring of the perceptions of the children with whom they work. Agencies should also assess their own performance and that of their staff against principles and practice standards derived from evaluation interviews with children in receipt of their services.

8 Conclusion

In this book we have tried to present the un*adult*erated accounts of children and young people on some subjects that are of serious, mutual interest to them and to the adults in their lives. We felt that we needed to do so having considered some of the many reasons why the views of children and young people do not usually find their way into the serious councils of the adult world. We have suggested that there is a cultural predisposition to discount the views of children and young people that is built on a deficit model of childhood, constructed to satisfy the unmet needs of adults. In doing so, we do not intend to argue that the interests of children and adults are so very widely divergent, certainly not as divergent as the 'child liberationists' might want us to believe.

We do suggest differences however, in style and substance between the social worlds of adults and those of young people. Some of these differences are not adequately reflected in the thin literature on research in this field and we have attempted to record some of the difficulties that we encountered in pursuing the research this book reports in the hope that we and others might do better next time.

We do have to find better ways to communicate effectively across the generations, particularly in regard to troubled and vulnerable children. We suspected that many of the children and young people we worked with in our professional lives were moving further away from where we were. This suspicion prompted the research in the first place. We are now, sadly, and perhaps, more wisely, even more concerned to find so many young people with little or no faith in the adults around them. They doubt our commitment. They doubt our understanding and they doubt our capacity to be of any use to them when they need us most. And they have a point.

In writing this book, we wanted to see the concern that adults feel for children, albeit generated partly for our own purposes, used to serve the interests of children and young people better. To do that we do need to talk and, perhaps even more importantly, we do need to listen, respect and learn from what they have to say to us.

We have tried to show how young people's idea of 'safe' can be allied to our adult idea of 'protection', to the mutual advantage of both. We may have to expand our organisational priorities as well as our professional practice to do so and even take more risks in the short term. But as well as the children who we can bureaucratically account for as 'at risk', we believe there are others equally 'at risk' who we will never get to hear about. The consequences for them are real too. We do not in any sense denigrate the expertise and commitment of those who are working for children and young people but our professional record, particularly in social work, is not a particularly distinguished one. This is only one example. Each of us, in our own professional spheres could profit from seeking to ground what we do in the realities of the lives of the young people in whose name we collect our pay and develop our services accordingly.

If the book has caused you to find out what a child close to you is thinking about what you do, it will have served its purpose.

Bibliography

Adler, P. and Adler, P. (1978) 'Tinydopers: a case study of deviant socialization', *Symbolic Interaction* 1, 90–105.

Andrews, C. (1980) 'Is blood thicker than local authorities?' *Social Work Today* 12(1) 2 September 1980 19–21.

Archard, D. (1993) *Children — Rights and Childhood* London: Routledge.

Aries, P. (1960) *L'Enfant et la vie familiale sous l'ancien regime* Paris: Libraire Plon. Translated by Robert Baldick as *Centuries of Childhood* (1962) London: Jonathan Cape.

Arnstein, R. (1972) 'Power to the people: an assessment of the community action and model cities experience' *Public Administration Review* 32.

Atherton, C. and Dowling, P. (1989) 'Using written agreements: the family's point of view' in Aldgate, J. (ed.) *Using Written Agreements with Children and Families* London: Family Rights Group.

Ayalon, O. and Flasher, A. (1993) *Chain Reaction: Children and Divorce* London: Jessica Kingsley.

Bamford, T. (1990) *The Future of Social Work* London: MacMillan.

Bannister, A., Barrett, K. and Shearer, E. (eds) (1990) *Listening to Children: The Professional Response to Hearing the Abused Child* London: Longman.

Biestek, F. (1961) *The Casework Relationship* London: Allen and Unwin.

Billis, D. (1984) *Welfare Bureaucracies: Their Design and Change in Response to Social Problems* London: Heinemann.

Blackburn, C. (1991) *Poverty and Health: Working with Families* Milton Keynes: Open University Press.

Blagg, H., Hughes, J. and Wattam, C. (eds) (1989) *Child Sexual Abuse: Listening, Hearing and Validating the Experiences of Children* London: Longman/NSPCC.

Bolton, F. G., Morris, L. A. and Maceachron, A. E. (1989) *Males at Risk: the other side of child sexual abuse* Newbury Park CA. USA: Sage.

Brake, M. (1980) *The Sociology of Youth Culture and Youth Subcultures* London: Routledge and Kegan Paul.

Broady, M. and Hedley, R. (1989) *Working Partnerships: Community Development in Local Authorities* London: Bedford Square Press.

Buchanan, A. (ed.) (1994) *Partnership in Practice* Aldershot: Avebury.

Butler, I. and Owens, D. (1993) 'Canaries Among Sparrows —Ideas of the Family and the Practice of Foster Care' *International Journal of Family Care* 5, no. 25–42.

Butler-Sloss, E. (1988) (DHSS) *Report of the Inquiry into Child Abuse in Cleveland 1987* London: HMSO.

Cahill, M. (1994) *The New Social Policy* Oxford: Blackwell.

Carrington, B. and Troyna, B. (eds) (1988) *Children and Controversial Issues* Lewes: Falmer.

Clyde, J. J. (1992) *Report of the Inquiry into the Removal of Children from Orkney in February 1991* Edinburgh: HMSO.

Coffield, F., Borrill, C. and Marshall, S. (1986) *Growing Up and the Margins: Young Adults in the North-East* Milton Keynes: Open University Press.

Coit, K. (1978) 'Local action not citizen participation', in Tabb, W. and Sawers, L. (eds) *Marxism and the Metropolis* New York: Oxford University Press.

Coleman, J. and Hendry, L. (1990) *The Nature of Adolescence* 2nd edn, London: Routledge.

Coles, R. (1967) *Children of Crisis* Boston USA: Little, Brown.

Coles, R. (1986) *The Moral Life of Children* Boston USA: Houghton Mifflin.

Covington, L. and Beery, R. (1977) *Self-worth and School Learning* New York: Reinhart & Winston.

Darvill, G. and Smale, G. (eds) (1990) *Partners in Empowerment: Networks of Innovation in Social Work* London: National Institute for Social Work.

Davies, M. (1985) *The Essential Social Worker — A Guide to Positive Practice*, Aldershot: Gower.

Davis, J. (1990) *Youth and the Condition of Britain: Images of Adolescent Conflict* London: Athlone.

Dembo, R., Williams, L. *et al.* (1992), 'A structural model examining the relationship between physical child abuse, sexual victimization, and marijuana/hashish use in delinquent youth: a longitudinal study' *Violence and Victims* 7 No. 1: 41–62.

Denzin, N. K. (1977) *Childhood Socialization* San Francisco: Jossey-Bass.

DES (1982) *Young People in the 1980s* London: HMSO.

Dewar, J. (1989) 2nd Edn (1992) *Law and the Family*, London: Butterworths.

DHSS (1985) *Social Work Decisions in Child Care: Recent Research Findings and their Implications* London: HMSO.

Directors of Social Work in Scotland (1992) *Child Protection: Policy, Practice and Procedure* Edinburgh: HMSO.

Dobash, R. (1977) The relationship between violence directed at women and violence directed at children within the family setting, Appendices to the *Minutes of Evidence* taken before the House of Commons parliamentary select committee on violence in the family, London: HMSO.

Dobash, R. and Dobash, R. (1992) *Women, Violence and Social Change* London: Routledge.

DOH (1988) *Protecting Children: A Guide for Social Workers undertaking a Comprehensive Assessment* London: HMSO.

DOH (1989) *An Introduction to the Children Act 1989* London: HMSO.

DOH (1991a) *Child Abuse: A Study of Inquiry Reports 1980–1989* London: HMSO.

DOH (1991b) *The Children Act 1989 Guidance and Regulations: Volume 1, Court Orders* London: HMSO.

DOH (1991c) *Patterns and Outcomes in Child Placement: Messages from Current Research and their Implications* London: HMSO.

Dolphin Project, The (1994) 'The Voice of the Child: Report by Young People on the Children Act 1989' in Buchanan, A. (ed.) *Partnership in Practice: The Children Act 1989* Aldershot: Avebury.

Donzelot, J. (1977) *La Police des Familles, Les Editions de Minuit* Paris; Translated as *The Policing of Families: Welfare Versus the State* London: Hutchinson.

Eekelaar, J. (1991) *Regulating Divorce* London: Oxford University Press.

Elliot, F. (1986) *The Family: Change or Continuity?* Basingstoke: MacMillan.

Family Law (1994) *Children: Law and Practice* Update 5, para. C 125 ff.; Bristol: Family Law.

Family Rights Group (1991) *The Children Act 1989: Working in Partnership with Families* London: HMSO.

Feminist Review (1988) 'Family Secrets: Child Sexual Abuse' Special Issue No. 28.

Fine, G. (1981) 'Friends, Impression Management and Pre-adolescent Behaviour', in Asher, S. and Gottman, J. (eds) *The Development of Children's Friendships* Cambridge: Cambridge University Press.

Fine, G. (1987) *With the Boys* Chicago: Chicago Press.

Fine, G. and Sandstrom, K. (1988) *Knowing Children — Participant Observation with Minors* Newbury Park CA USA: Sage.

Finkelhor, D., Gelles, R., Hotaling, G. and Straus, M. (eds) (1983) *The Dark Side of Families* Newbury Park, CA USA: Sage.

Firestone, S. (1979) 'Childhood is Hell', in Hoyles, M. (ed.) (1979) *Changing Childhood* London: Writers and Readers Publishing Co-operative.

Flekkoy, M. (1991) *A Voice for Children: Speaking Out as their Ombudsman* London: Jessica Kingsley.

Fontaine, J. (1991) *Bullying: The Child's View* London: Calouste Gulbenkian Foundation.

Fox Harding, L. (1991) *Perspectives in Child Care Policy* London: Longman.

Frankenburg, S. (1934) *Common Sense in the Nursery* London: Cape.

Franklin, B. (ed.) (1986) *The Rights of Children* London: Blackwell.

Freeman, M. (1983) 'Freedom and the welfare state: childrearing, parental autonomy and state intervention' *Journal of Social Welfare Law* March 1983, pp.70–91.

Freeman, M. (1992) *Children, Their Families and the Law: Working with the Children Act* London: MacMillan.

Furniss, T. (1991) *The Multi-professional Handbook of Child Sexual Abuse* London: Routledge.

Gibbons, K. (1990) *Ellen Foster* New York, NY: Vintage Books.

Gilkes, J. (1989) 'Coming to terms with sexual abuse: a day care perspective' in Riches, P. (ed.) *Responses to Cleveland: Improving Services for Child Sexual Abuse* London: Whiting and Birch/National Children's Bureau.

Gill, K. and Pickles, T. (1989) *Active Collaboration: Joint Practice and Youth Strategies* Glasgow: ITRC.

Goffman, E. (1961) *Asylums* New York: Doubleday.

Hadley, R. and McGrath, M. (eds) (1980) *Going Local: Neighbourhood Social Services* London: Bedford Square Press.

Hall, S. and Jefferson, T. (1978) *Resistance through Rituals* London: Hutchinson.

Havighurst, R. (1972) *Developmental Tasks and Education* New York: McKay.

Hendricks, J., Black, D. and Kaplan, T. (1993) *When Father Kills Mother: Guiding Children through Trauma and Grief* London: Routledge.

Hendry, L., Shucksmith, J., Love, J. and Glendinning, A. (1993) *Young People's Leisure and Lifestyles* London: Routledge.

Herbert, C. (1989) *Talking of Silence: The Sexual Harassment of Schoolgirls* London: Falmer.

Heywood, J. S. (1969) *Childhood and Society 100 Years Ago* London: National Children's Home.

HO/DOH (1991) *Working Together Under the Children Act 1989* London: HMSO.

HO/DOH (1992) *Memorandum of Good Practice on Video Recorded Interviews with Child Witnesses for Criminal Proceedings* London: HMSO.

Holman, R. (1980) 'A real child care policy for the future' *Community Care* 18/25 December 1980, 340, 16–17.

Holman, R. (1981) *Kids at the Door* Oxford: Basil Blackwell.

Holman, R. (1983) *Resourceful Friends: Skills in Community Social Work* London: The Children's Society.

Holman, R. (1988) *Putting Families First: Prevention and Child Care* London: Macmillan.

Holt, J. (1975) *Escape from Childhood. The Needs and Rights of Children* London: Penguin.

Howe D. (1987) *An Introduction to Social Work Theory* Aldershot: Wildwood House.

Howe, D. (1990) 'The Client's View in Context', in Carter, P., Jeffs, T. and Smith, M. (eds) *Social Work and Social Welfare Yearbook 3* Milton Keynes: Open University Press.

Hoyles, M. (1989) *The Politics of Childhood* London: Journeyman.

Hutchinson R. (1994) 'Partnership and the Children Act 1989' in Buchanan, A. (ed.) *Partnership in Practice* Aldershot: Avebury.

Johnson, T. (1972) *Professions and Power* London: MacMillan.

Kaplan, H. (1980) *Deviant Behaviour in Defense of Self* New York: Academic Press.

Kelly, A. (1991) 'The "new" managerialism in the social services' in Carter, P., Jeffs, T. and Smith, M. (eds) *Social Work and Social Welfare: Yearbook 3* Milton Keynes: Open University Press.

Kittrie, N. (1971) *The Right to Be Different: Deviance and Enforced Therapy* Baltimore: John Hopkins Press.

Laing, R. (1969) *The Politics of the Family* Canada: CPC Publications.

Laing, R. and Esterson, A. (1964) *Sanity, Madness and the Family* London: Tavistock.

Langan, M. and Lee, P. (1989) *Radical Social Work Today* London: Unwin Hyman.

Lorenz, W. (1993) *Social Work in a Changing Europe* London: Routledge.

Mac an Ghaill, M. (1994) *The Making of Men: Masculinities, Sexualities and Schooling* Buckingham: Open University Press.

Mandell, N. (1988) 'The Least-Adult Role in Studying Children' *Journal of Contemporary Ethnography* **16**, 433–467.

Marsh, C. (1988) *The Survey Method* London: Allen and Unwin.

Marsh, P. and Fisher, M. (1992) *Good Intentions: Developing Partnership in the Social Services* York: Joseph Rowntree Foundation.

Martinson, F. (1981) 'Preadolescent Sexuality — Latent or Manifest?' in Constantine, L. and Martinson, F. M. *Children and Sex* Boston: Little, Brown.

Mayer, J. E. and Timms, N. (1970) *The Client Speaks: Working Class Impressions of Casework* London: Routledge and Kegan Paul.

McCarthy, M. (1989) 'Personal social services' in McCarthy, M. (ed.) *The New Politics of Welfare: An Agenda for the 1990s?*, London: Macmillan.

McCracken, G. (1988) *The Long Interview* Newbury Park CA. USA: Sage.

McGuire, P. and Daniel, S. (1972) *The Paint House: Words from an East End gang* London: Penguin.

Medrich, E., Roizen, J., Rubin, V. and Buckley, S. (1982) *The Serious Business of Growing Up: A study of children's lives outside school* London: University of California Press.

Morgan, S. and Righton, P. (eds) (1989) *Child Care: Concerns and Conflicts* London: Hodder and Stoughton.

Muncie, J (1984) *The Trouble with Kids Today — Youth and Crime in Post-war Britain* London: Hutchinson.

National Institute of Justice (1992) *New Approaches to Interviewing Children: A Test of Its Effectiveness* Research in Brief, Washington: National Institute of Justice.

OPCS (1992) *Social Trends* London: HMSO.

Parton, N. (1991) *Governing the Family* London: Macmillan.

Pearson, G. (1983) *Hooligan. A History of Respectable Fears* London: Macmillan.

Phelan, J. (1983) *Family Centres: A Study* London: The Children's Society.

Pinchbeck, I. and Hewitt, M. (1973) *Children in English Society* London: Routledge and Kegan Paul.

Pitt-Aikens, T. and Thomas Ellis, A. (1990) *Loss of the Good Authority: The Cause of Delinquency* London: Viking.

Pollock, L. (1983) *Forgotten Children. Parent–child relations from 1500–1900* Cambridge: Cambridge University Press.

Rees, G. (1993) *Hidden Truths: Young People's Experience of Running Away* London: The Children's Society.

Reid, J. (1986) *'You've Got to Rebel': The exercise of authority in work with young adults* Bedford: Cranfield Press.

Robins, D. and Cohen, P. (1978) *Knuckle Sandwich — Growing up in the Working-class City* London: Penguin.

Rogers, W., Hevey, D. and Ash, E. (eds) (1989) *Child Abuse and Neglect: Facing the Challenge* London: Batsford.

Runciman, W. (1972) *Relative Deprivation and Social Justice* Harmondsworth: Penguin.

Rutter, M. and Rutter, M. (1992) *Developing Minds: Change and Continuity Across the Life-Span* London: Penguin.

Short Report (1984) *Second Report from the Social Services Committee: Children in Care* 1 London: HMSO.

Skinner, A. (1992) *Bullying: An annotated bibliograpy of literature and resources* Leicester: Youth Work Press.

Stainton-Rogers, W. and Worrel, M. (eds) (1993) *Investigative Interviewing with Children* Milton Keynes: Open University Press.

Stanley Hall, G. (1904) *Adolescence* New York: Appleton.

Stanley, B. and Sieber, J. (1992) *Social Research on Children and Adolescents — Ethical Issues* Newbury Park CA USA: Sage.

Stone, M. (1993) *Child Protection: A Model for Risk Assessment in Physical Abuse/Neglect* Surrey: Surrey County Council.

Strathdee, R. (1993) *Housing Our Children* London: Centrepoint Soho.

Takii, Y. (1992) 'Sexual Abuse and Juvenile Delinquency' *Child Abuse Review* 1, No. 1, 43–48.

Tattum, D. (ed.) (1993) *Understanding and Managing Bullying* London: Trentham Books.

Tattum, D. and Lane, D. (eds) (1988) *Bullying in Schools* London: Trentham Books.

Townsend, P. (1979) *Poverty in the United Kingdom* Harmondsworth: Penguin.

Troyna, B. and Hatcher, R. (1992) *Racism in Children's Lives: A Study of Mainly White Primary Schools* London: Routledge.

UNICEF (1991) *The State of the World's Children* Oxford: Oxford University Press.

Van Every, J. (1992) 'Who is the family? The assumptions of British social policy' *Critical Social Policy* 33, 62–75.

Varma, V. (ed.) (1992) *The Secret Life of Vulnerable Children* London: Routledge.

Waksler, F. (ed.) (1991) *Studying the Social Worlds of Children: Sociological Readings* London: Falmer.

Walter, J. (1978) *Sent Away: a Study of Young Offenders in Care* Farnborough: Saxon House.

Williamson, H. (1981) *Juvenile Justice and the Working Class Community* unpublished Ph.D thesis, Cardiff: University of Wales.

Williamson, H. (1985) 'Struggling Beyond Youth' *Youth in Society* January, 11–12.

Williamson, H. (1993) 'Youth policy and the marginalisation of young people' *Youth and Policy* No. 40, 33–48.

Williamson, H. and Weatherspoon, K. (1985) *Strategies for Intervention: an Approach to Youth and Community Work in an Area of Social Deprivation* Cardiff: University College Cardiff, Social Research Unit.

Willis, P. (1978) *Learning to Labour: How Working Class Kids get Working Class Jobs* Farnborough: Saxon House.